Feasts of Veg

Vibrant Vegetarian Recipes for Gatherings

———

Nina Olsson

An Hachette UK Company
www.hachette.co.uk

First published in Great Britain in 2018 by
Kyle Books, an imprint of Kyle Cathie Ltd
Carmelite House
50 Victoria Embankment
London EC4Y 0DZ
www.kylebooks.co.uk

ISBN: 978 085783 447 8

Photographer, Stylist and Designer: Nina Olsson
Assisting stylists: Sarah Cheikh, Nova Olsson, Bensimon
Van Leyen, Fleur Schouten, and Santouscha Tjietaman
Project Editor: Sophie Allen
Copy Editor: Jo Richardson
Editorial assistant: Sarah Kyle
Production: Nic Jones, Gemma John and Lisa Pinnell

A Cataloguing in Publication record for this title is available from the
British Library.

Contents

Sharing the Goodness

This book is filled with vegetarian recipes for dinners, gatherings and parties. It's the kind of food I like to eat myself and to serve to friends and family. There's no more beautiful meal to share than a feast with vibrant vegetables, whether it's a golden roasted root gratin with mushrooms or a sparkling rainbow-coloured salad. This book is about sharing good food, one of the most enjoyable things to do in life.

A great feast raises our spirits and you can actually say it's a form of wellness activity, so there's no need to feel indulgent for throwing the occasional party – you're sharing the goodness.

When I was too young to join in with my parents' dinner parties, my siblings and I would fall asleep to the muddled sound of laughter and music. I remember feeling excited, thinking this must be the best part of being a grown up, celebrating together, filling the house with food and friends. And when I pictured my older self, I saw myself cooking and hosting my own dinner parties. I still feel that excitement, especially when the cooking is done for the night and I can sit down with my guests at the table, enjoy a drink and let the magic of the evening unfold.

My mother, who was a housewife in the seventies, preferred to put textiles and paint canvases before household duties, but she would go all out to make our celebrations memorable. One of the most cherished memories I have is from my seventh birthday, sitting at the head of a long table set on the grass with my friends, surrounded by lilac bushes in the high summer afternoon, with a layered strawberry cake, flowers and lemonade. The love and effort my mum put into arranging this simple but unforgettable day, is my measuring stick for hosting today. My birthday happens to coincide with midsummer, which maybe adds to why I think it's the best holiday of the year. The feasts of our lives become memories in a timeline that we can see our own life stories through. At the heart of every feast there's a place, people and good food.

Vegetables are the stars in this book and now is a really exciting time to be a vegetarian. The art of cooking vegetables is undergoing a renaissance, and there's virtually an army of creative chefs, authors and bloggers all making a new style of vegetarianism

happen. In my opinion, talking about vegetables and vegetarian food as a meat substitute feels outdated today. It's not about 'if' we should eat plant-based today, it's more a question of 'how'. And my own answer to that is to focus on flavour and take inspiration from world kitchens, to think outside the box and use techniques that can utilise the various textures and flavours of vegetables. The creative possibilities are vast. I can think of no better way to celebrate the future of food than by serving vegetables.

Setting the scene

A good party can be a grand spectacle or as simple as a picnic in the park. In the end it's the spirit that we bring into it that matters. People, not furniture, make the party. A beautifully styled table with fine tableware and professional flower arrangements can be the stuff of lifelong memories, but it doesn't mean it's more enjoyable than a pot-luck gathering on the beach, grilling veggie burgers with the sun setting.

If you are hosting in your home, simply adding candlelight and flowers to the equation can set the right mood. Mixing new with old and borrowed tableware is always charming.

Taking the party outdoors, eating al fresco, out in nature is fantastic: take chairs, tables and why not rugs, pouffes and sofas to create a fabulous outdoor scene. Build a fire (in a safe manner!) and hang lamps or light lanterns between trees.

How to host a gathering

Gatherings are becoming increasingly casual in general – it's more about making sure there's a relaxed welcoming atmosphere for the guests to enjoy, thus, so don't stress. Forget about perfection or following strict etiquette!

So now you have set a date and invited a number of people, here are some pointers on how to throw a great dinner:

• **Being a relaxed host** is essential! Get organised, make a plan and prepare as much as you can in advance.

• **Check in advance if any guests** have allergies or special diets and make adjustments accordingly.

• **Create atmosphere,** light candles, make a music play list, buy flowers and rearrange furniture and declutter the space if it needs it.

• **Balance your menu,** don't feed your guests too much bread, nibbles or heavy starters if your main dish is the star dish on the menu. If everyone is getting full before you serve it, they won't appreciate your effort. Hunger is the best spice!

• **Make sure there's ice in the freezer** for drinks. And make sure there's enough glasses.

• **Have a wabi-sabi approach,** if something goes wrong, be light about it and move on.

• **Don't be overambitious.** Don't choose to cook several complicated dishes for one dinner, if you're cooking alone. Choose one more demanding dish to impress with and keep the rest simple. Or get someone to help.

• **It's always a good idea** to involve others to help – usually your partner or good friends. Delegate responsibility for dishes to others, or let them manage the music and bar, or have them making sure the dishwasher is emptied and filled between servings.

• **Also, make sure** guests are not excluded from conversation; if someone is being ignored try to draw them into the dynamic.

Get organised

Prepare what you can in advance so that you only need to finish the final steps of cooking a dish when guests have arrived. And remember that not every dish has to be homemade; it's perfectly fine to serve a quality chocolate, storebought ice cream or fruit after a main dish.

Make a plan and shop in advance.
Can be prepared a week ahead:
Jams, confit, chutney and ice cream.
Can be prepared a few days ahead:
Go through plates, tablecloths, glasses and napkins and wash or replace as needed.
Can be prepared a day ahead:
Stews, curries and soups. Store in the fridge and warm up just before serving. Leaving a stew to sit makes the flavours intensify and taste even better.
Cold sauces, marinades, dressings, nut and seaweed sprinkles can also be prepared a day ahead.
Cakes, bread, pizza dough and cookies can be prepared hours or a day ahead. For layer cakes, assemble and spread on the filling and icing just before serving.
Veggies that need to be roasted, fried or grilled can be cut and marinated the day before.
Patties, sausages and croquettes can be mixed and shaped and placed in the fridge a day ahead. Fry or grill just before serving.
Pasta can be prepared a day head. Store in the fridge and cook just before serving.
Syrups for cocktails can be mixed a day ahead.
Can be prepared hours earlier on the same day:
Make salads on the same day. It tastes delicious the fresher it's made so ideally no more than 2–3 hours before serving.

Before you start cooking, prepare your mise en place. Mise en place is a French expression for placing out all you need on the work surface before you start.

How to use this book

All dishes can be freely combined to create a menu. I have mostly used organic ingredients where possible.

Most recipes are sufficient to serve four people; simply multiply amounts for bigger parties.

Always taste the food before serving and adjust with salt to taste, or if applicable, the amount of lemon juice, chilli, or extra virgin olive oil. I always salt carefully to allow guests to salt to their own taste.

If you are on a sugar-free diet, omit sugars from the recipe.

If you don't use coconut products, substitute with suitable replacement. Use other vegetable oil instead of coconut oil, vegan or dairy cooking cream instead of coconut milk.

Soy sauce: In this book I refer to soy sauce as shoyu, the japanese name for soy sauce. Many soy sauces sold in supermarkets are made in China and often are made with artificial colouring, molasses and are not fermented, which is the traditonal and more healthy way to consumer soy. Japanese soy is far more often fermented, so to be extra sure of getting a quality soy, or shoyu, shop at a natural food store.

Herbs: Fresh delicate herbs like tarragon, basil, parsley, coriander and mint are interchangeable with each other but will alter the flavour. Bear in mind that mint adds quite a strong character. Sturdier herbs such as rosemary and thyme are easily interchangeable.

Grains are easily substituted with each other, just adjust cooking times and the amount of cooking liquids accordingly.

Sweeteners: I use honey or agave syrup as liquid sweeteners and coconut sugar, or brown sugar where crystallised sugar is required. I use the same sweeteners out of convenience. You can easily substitute honey and agave for maple or other sweet liquid sweeteners, or, if you use stevia, adjust the amount used accordingly.

Hot sauces: Chilli sauces have different characteristics, and there's a variety used in the book. You can substitute other chilli sauces and finely chopped fresh chilli pepper.

Vegan: Where butter or ghee is listed, use vegetable oil instead. For dairy and egg products, use vegan substitutes. Suggestions are given with each recipe.

Gluten free: Suggestions are given with each recipe.

Substitutes

Most ingredients can be substituted with similar ingredients. As an example, if a recipe lists cavolo nero (black cabbage) as an ingredient you can easily substitute with kale. Squashes and pumpkins are interchangeable, red onion with other onions, and so on.

'A good cook is like a sorceress who dispenses happiness.'

ELSA SCHIAPARELLI

Quick canapé ideas:
sliced cucumber topped
with red pesto and
red romaine salad
filled with hummus
and topped with
pomegranate seeds.

1. SMALL BITES

These tempting nibbles and small servings are for serving to your guests
when they first arrive at your gathering, to satisfy their immediate hunger
but also to excite their appetites and expectations for what's to come.
Although these little dishes are designed to kick off the proceedings,
you can also mix and match them with dishes from other chapters
in the book, in either single or several servings.
Now let's get this party started!

Okonomiyaki

MAKES 4 PANCAKES; SERVES 4

400g radicchio or white cabbage, very
    finely shredded (or other finely
    shredded cabbage or finely grated
    vegetables – see recipe introduction)
2 spring onions, thinly sliced
2 tablespoons finely chopped pickled
    ginger or 1 tablespoon ground ginger
50ml dashi or water
4 medium organic eggs, lightly beaten
250g plain flour
1 teaspoon baking powder
salt, to taste
sesame or vegetable oil, for frying

OKONOMIYAKI SAUCE:

50ml Worcestershire sauce
50ml tomato ketchup
50ml shoyu soy or tamari sauce

TO SERVE:

mayonnaise or kewpie mayonnaise
furikake (see page 166 for homemade)
extra shredded cabbage (radicchio
    for topping)

Okonomiyaki **translates from the Japanese literally as 'how you want it',
which means that this pancake recipe can be easily customised to your
liking. Choose your favourite cabbage or other finely grated vegetables,
like potato, beetroot, courgette and radishes.**

———

Mix together the ingredients for the onomiyaki sauce in a small bowl. For the
pancakes, put the cabbage, spring onions, ginger, dashi or water and beaten
eggs in a large bowl and mix together until the vegetables are evenly coated
with the egg. Sprinkle the flour and baking powder over the vegetable mixture
and mix together, seasoning with salt.

Heat a frying pan that has a lid to a medium-high heat – the pancakes can
easily burn, so take care that the pan doesn't get too hot. Drizzle the base of
the pan with oil, then spoon in a quarter of the pancake mixture and swirl the
pan to make a pancake about 15cm in diameter. Fry for about a minute until it
begins to firm. Cover the pan with the lid and continue cooking the pancake
for 1–2 minutes until the underside is nicely browned. To flip the pancake,
hold the lid firmly against the pan and invert the pan and lid together so that
the pancake transfers to the lid. Lift the pan away and then carefully slide
the pancake from the lid back into the pan with the browned side up. Fry for
1–2 minutes until the other side is golden brown, then slide onto a warmed
plate. Repeat with the remainder of the pancake mixture.

Serve the pancakes warm with the okonomiyaki sauce, mayonnaise
and furikake.

VE Opt for egg replacer, and vegan Worcestershire sauce
and mayonnaise; make your own furikake (see page 166)
or look for tuna-free furikake if buying ready-made.
GF Check the contents of the baking powder to ensure
that it's gluten free; opt for tamari sauce.

Hurricane Popcorn

SERVES 4
50g butter or 3 tablespoons vegetable oil
½ teaspoon shoyu soy or tamari sauce
100g popping corn
salt, to taste (optional)

HURRICANE FURIKAKE SEASONING:
1 nori sheet, toasted and cut with scissors
  into very fine strips (plus a few extra
  strips, to garnish)
50g sesame seeds
2 tablespoons shoyu soy or tamari sauce
½ tablespoon shichimi togarashi or dried
  chilli flakes
1 tablespoon coconut sugar

When I heard about this Hawaiian-style popcorn, I knew I would love it. Firstly, it fuses East and West by using the Japanese spice mix furikake, traditionally added to rice and other Japanese foods for a umami boost, to season good old popcorn. But to make it even more interesting, it also mixes savoury and sweet flavours – always a winning combination – by adding a touch of coconut sugar to the seaweed and sesame-based furikake to give the popcorn a highly addictive funky flavour. Shichimi togarashi is a Japanese chilli-based spice mix, which you can buy from well-stocked supermarkets, along with nori sheets, or from Asian supermarkets or online suppliers. Thanks Hawaii!

Put all the ingredients for the furikake seasoning in a food processor and whizz until well combined.

Prepare the popcorn shortly before serving to enjoy at its best. Heat a large saucepan that has a tight-fitting lid over a high heat. Add the butter or oil, soy and corn, then shake the pan so that all kernels are coated with the melted butter or oil. Cover the pan with the lid and cook until the sound of the corn popping has just stopped.

Transfer the popcorn to a bowl, add the furikake seasoning, and salt to taste if you like, and toss to mix. It's now ready to serve.

VE Opt for vegetable oil.
GF Opt for tamari sauce.

Pop it!

There's been a huge trend of new creative popcorn brands offering exciting new flavours to taste. But of course nothing beats home-popped corn and you can easily create state of the art popcorn with various flavours at home. Try nutritional yeast, lingonberry powder, cinnamon, salty caramel chocolate, wasabi powder, za'atar, dill or Parmesan for a delicious twist!

From the top left:
Hurricane Popcorn, furikake
seasoning and natural popcorn
sprinkled with lingonberry powder
and coconut sugar.

Hot Aubergine Crisps

Feel like serving something a bit more adventurous than potato crisps from a bag? These homemade aubergine alternatives are the perfect solution!

SERVES 10

1 teaspoons shichimi togarashi
1 teaspoon salt, or to taste
4 small aubergines, thinly sliced lengthways
toasted sesame oil, for brushing
2 small handfuls of panko breadcrumbs

RED PEPPER MISO DIP

1 roasted red pepper from a jar, drained
1 garlic clove, crushed
2 tablespoons red or brown miso
1 teaspoon sesame oil
2 tablespoons rice vinegar
water, to thin
salt, to taste

Preheat the oven to 180°C/gas mark 4. Line two large baking trays with baking paper. Mix together the shichimi togarashi and salt. Arrange the aubergine slices in a single layer on the lined trays. Brush with the toasted sesame oil and sprinkle with the spicy salt mix. Sprinkle with panko breadcrumbs. Bake for 15 minutes, then flip the slices over and bake for a further 5 minutes or until golden and crisp.

Meanwhile, to make the dip, blend all the ingredients together in a food processor. Add small amounts of water until you achieve the desired consistency. Adjust with salt, to taste. Serve immediately.

VE ✓
GF Chose gluten-free breadcrumbs or omit the panko breadcrumbs.

Kale Crisps and Lemony Cashew Cream

These crisps are featherlight and crispy. Add za'atar or another spice for extra interest. The lemony cashew cream is one of my all-time favourite dips – dairy free and full of flavour.

SERVES 4

LEMONY CASHEW CREAM:

3 tablespoons cashew butter
juice of ½ lemon
2 tablespoons extra virgin olive oil
pinch of salt
1 garlic clove
1 teaspoon honey
3 tablespoons almond milk

KALE CRISPS:

500g green or black cabbage (Savoy or cavolo nero), cut into small pieces, stems removed
1 tablespoon olive oil, for baking
1½ tablespoons za'atar spice mix
pinch of salt

Preheat the oven to 200°C/gas mark 6 and line a baking tray with baking paper.

For the lemony cashew cream, mix the dip ingredients in a bowl and set aside until ready to serve.

For the crisps, add the cabbage to a bowl. Drizzle with the olive oil and sprinkle with za'atar and salt mix to get an even coating of oil and spice. Place on a papered tray and bake for 15–20 minutes – keep a close eye to avoid burning. Let it cool and serve with the cashew cream

VE ✓
GF ✓

Sweet Potato Crisps

Wholesome, but with a decadent feel, these colourful homemade crisps will be a favourite snack!

SERVES 4

2–3 sweet potatoes, peeled and sliced
1 tablespoon olive oil, for baking
pinch of salt
1 tablespoon apple cider vinegar

TO SERVE

Lemony Cashew Cream (see left)

Preheat the oven to 150°C/gas mark 3 and line a baking tray with baking paper.

For the sweet potato crisps, add the slices to a bowl and mix with olive oil, apple cider vinegar and salt. Place on the lined tray and sprinkle with cinnamon. Bake in the oven for 20 minutes. It's important to keep an eye on them to decide if they are done – the crisps should curl up and be fairly dry. Let them cool and serve with the lemony cashew cream.

VE ✓
GF ✓

Onigiri

SERVES 8
300g Japanese or sushi rice (round,
    short-grained white rice)
360ml water
½ teaspoon salt
2 tablespoons black sesame seeds
5 x 1cm long nori ribbons (cut from
    a sheet of nori)

PICKLES:
vegetables, such as carrot, beetroot and
    cabbage or other greens
ume-su or rice vinegar
salt, to taste

For the orange onigiri I used pickled
    carrots and umeboshi plums
For the green onigiri I used picked and
    massaged kale, spring onions, fresh
    coriander and umeboshi plums
For the pink onigiri I used pickled
    radicchio, red onion, shiso leaf
    seasoning and umeboshi plums

OTHER FLAVOURING/FILLING OPTIONS:
crumbled smoked tofu mixed with
    wasabi-flavoured mayonnaise
spring onions, finely chopped
furikake (see page 166 for homemade)
nori
black sesame seeds
shiso leaf seasoning

Tip

*You will find shiso leaf seasoning in many
well-stocked supermarkets or, if not, in
Asian supermarkets or online, where
you will also be able to source ume-su
(umeboshi plum vinegar). Japanese or sushi
rice isn't a specific variety of rice but refers
to a type of round, short-grained rice,
which is slightly sticky when cooked.*

**Onigiri, Japanese rice balls, are often sold in Japanese delis and are a
staple of the traditional Japanese bento lunch box. Even if you haven't
yet tasted onigiri, you may well have seen the onigiri emojis, a sign of
their rising popularity in the world. They are fun to make and can easily
be varied with all kinds of flavourings and fillings, although I like to stick
to typical Japanese ingredients – a mixture of furikake seasoning and
pickles. The seasoning and fillings can either be mixed through the rice
or used as a stuffing for the rice.**

To prepare the pickles, if you want to use them for flavouring/filling your
onigiri, peel where appropriate and roughly chop the vegetables and/or shiso
leaves, then put them in a ceramic or glass bowl. Pour over ume-su or rice
vinegar to cover and leave to stand at room temperature for 30 minutes.
Massage the marinated vegetables for 2 minutes, then drain and chop very
finely.

Put the rice in a sieve and rinse in several changes of cold water until the
water is clear. Tip the drained rice into a saucepan that has a tight-fitting lid,
stir in the measured water and salt and bring to the boil. Reduce to a simmer,
cover the pan with the lid and cook for 20 minutes. Turn off the heat and
leave the rice to steam, with the lid on, for about 10 minutes. Then uncover
and leave the rice to cool slightly, but it should still be warm when you form
the onigiri.

You can now choose to stir the cooked rice through the prepared pickled
vegetables or herbs and/or microgreens or any other flavourings, such as
umeboshi plums, smoked tofu and wasabi mayo, fresh herbs or spring onions
or furikake. Any ingredient you want to mix through the rice needs to be
chopped very finely. Alternatively, leave the rice as it is for stuffing once you
have formed the onigiri.

Wet your hands and take a handful of rice. Gently press and mould the rice
with your hands to form a triangular shape. If you want to stuff the onigiri,
press your thumb into the rice to make a hollow in the centre, add your chosen
filling and re-shape the rice to enclose it. Sprinkle with the black sesame seeds
or shiso leaf seasoning, if using, and wrap each onigiri with a nori strip.

The fillings can be prepared two days ahead and kept, tightly covered or
in an airtight container, in the fridge. You can prepare the onigiri a day in
advance and keep, covered, in the fridge.

VE Opt for vegan mayonnaise; make your own furikake (see
page 166) or look for tuna-free furikake if buying ready-made.
GF Opt for gluten-free mayonnaise.

Summary Rolls with Satay Dip

MAKES 12

12 round rice paper sheets, plus a few extra in case of casualties

SATAY PEANUT DIPPING SAUCE:

3 tablespoons good-quality smooth peanut butter

2 tablespoons shoyu soy or tamari sauce

1 tablespoon lime juice

1 teaspoon grated fresh ginger

1 garlic clove, crushed

1 teaspoon agave syrup or coconut sugar

¼ teaspoon sriracha sauce

SALAD FILLING:

2 medium carrots, peeled and julienned or cut into thin matchsticks

a handful of mixed salad leaves (I use spinach and radicchio), torn or shredded

2 handfuls of finely shredded red cabbage

1 red or yellow pepper, cored, deseeded and cut into strips

1 small Chioggia beetroot, peeled and sliced into thin moons

1 small cucumber, cut into thin matchsticks

1 medium avocado, thinly sliced

4 spring onions, chopped

a handful of beansprouts

a handful of coriander

I remember when I took my first bite into a summer roll in a Vietnamese restaurant, and it was a revelation. I couldn't fathom how the taste could be so good when there was so little added flavouring apparent. I kept asking my food writer friend who ordered the rolls for me if he was sure there wasn't a hidden ingredient somewhere. Soon after, I bought rice papers and made my own rolls at home, stunned that they proved so easy to prepare and could taste so amazing. With summer rolls, there is only one clear rule in my opinion – while the salad ingredients can be flexible, the key ingredient that gives them that characteristic heavenly light clean taste is the coriander, so don't skip it! I just love this peanut sauce for dipping the rolls, but they are also delicious dipped into Japanese shoyu soy sauce (or tamari sauce for a wheat-free alternative) or simply toasted sesame oil and rice vinegar. Sriracha sauce, a Thai hot chilli sauce, is available from some Western supermarkets, Asian supermarkets or online suppliers.

Mix together all the ingredients for the satay peanut dipping sauce in a bowl. This can be prepared a day before serving and kept, tightly covered or in an airtight container, in the fridge.

The rolls are best enjoyed freshly made, so prepare just before guests arrive or let your guests make their own rolls.

Fill a bowl with lukewarm water. Dip a rice paper sheet in the water for 4–5 seconds. Transfer the rice paper to a work surface and wait a few seconds before adding the salad filling ingredients to the centre of it. Carefully fold the sides of the rice paper, which should now be pliable, over the filling snugly and then the bottom and top edges and roll up away from you, or you can leave the top edge open before rolling. Serve with the satay peanut dipping sauce.

VE ✓

GF Check the contents of the rice paper sheets to ensure that they are gluten free; opt for tamari sauce.

Tip

Want to make the rolls more substantial? Add 150–200g thin rice noodles, rehydrated according to the packet instructions and then rinsed in cold water and well drained, to the salad filling.

Butternut Squash Boats

SERVES 4

2 baby butternut squash, halved
  lengthways and seeds and
  membrane removed
olive oil, for drizzling
a generous handful of torn cavolo nero
  (black cabbage or kale), stems removed
caramelised nuts, crushed
salt and freshly ground black pepper,
  to taste

PUMPKIN SEED AND DATE CREAM:

2 tablespoons pumpkin seed butter
  or other nut butter, such as almond
  butter or tahini
2 Medjool dates, pitted
2 tablespoons lemon juice
1 tablespoon orange blossom water
  (optional)
¼ teaspoon ground chilli pepper
½ teaspoon salt
2 garlic cloves, crushed
50ml extra virgin olive oil

This is a delicious starter. The natural sweetness of the butternut squash is perfectly complemented by the nutty pumpkin seed and date cream, while the crispy cavolo nero and caramelised nuts add a lovely texture.

Preheat the oven to 200°C/gas mark 6. Line a large baking tray with baking paper. Arrange the butternut squash halves on the lined tray, cut side-down, drizzle with olive oil and season with salt and pepper. Bake for 30 minutes, then flip the halves over and bake for a further 10 minutes or until cooked through.

Mix the ingredients for the pumpkin seed and date cream in a food processor and whizz for a few seconds. Add small amounts of water until you reach your desired consistency. Transfer to a bowl and cover until serving. The cream can be prepared a day ahead and stored, sealed, in the fridge.

Heat a frying pan over a medium-high heat. Drizzle in a small amount of olive oil, add the cavolo nero and cook for about 1 minute, turning over halfway through, just until crispy but not burnt. Sprinkle with salt to taste.

Transfer the butternut squash boats to a platter. Top with the crispy cavolo nero. Sprinkle with crushed caramelised nuts and drizzle with the pumpkin seed and date cream.

VE ✓
GF ✓

Caramelised Onion Tarte Tatin

SERVES 8

SPELT PASTRY:
180g spelt flour
¼ teaspoon salt
125g butter, chilled, or coconut oil,
    soft but not liquid
about 2 tablespoons cold water

WHIPPED CHEESE:
200g fresh goat's cheese
½ tablespoon olive oil
sprinkle of salt

CARAMELISED ONIONS:
60g butter or 50ml olive oil, for frying
500g red onions or a mix of red onions
    and shallots, halved, trimmed and
    cut into wedges
2 teaspoons thyme leaves
2 tablespoons brown or coconut sugar
2 tablespoons red wine vinegar
salt, to taste

This beautiful pie is a riff on the classic sweet tarte tatin, an upside-down pastry tart traditionally made with apples, whereas I'm using naturally sweet onions for a savoury twist. Together with the salty crumbly pastry and whipped goat's cheese (or use vegan soft cheese), this makes a great addition to a table of small dishes. But if you are making it as a starring dish, it's delicious served with a fresh salad. You can use ready-made pastry dough instead of making the spelt pastry.

To make the pastry, mix together the flour and salt in a bowl. Add the butter or coconut oil in small pieces and rub it into the flour with your fingertips or work it in with a fork until evenly combined and the texture resembles breadcrumbs. Mix in the cold water to form a pliable mixture. Wrap in clingfilm and leave to rest in the fridge for 30 minutes. The pastry can be made 2–3 days in advance and stored, wrapped, in the fridge.

Meanwhile, preheat the oven to 190°C/gas mark 5. Put the ingredients for the whipped cheese in a bowl and whip until fluffy. Set aside and refrigerate until 15 minutes before serving.

Roll out the pastry between two sheets of baking paper into a sheet, roughly square, 1cm thick. Keep cool in the fridge until ready to use.

Heat a large ovenproof frying pan (about 20cm diameter) over a medium-high heat. Add the olive oil or butter, then arrange the onion wedges in a snug single layer in the pan. Season with salt and sprinkle with the thyme. Cover the pan with foil and bake in the oven for 35 minutes.

Remove from the oven, lift off the foil and sprinkle the sugar and vinegar over the onions. Cut a round from the pastry sheet slightly larger than the pan. Lay the pastry round over the onions and then tuck the edge in all round the inside of the pan to encase the onions. Bake for a further 20–25 minutes until the pastry is golden.

Remove the tart from the oven and leave to cool for a few minutes. Run a knife around the edge of the tart, then top the pan with a plate and, holding the plate firmly against the pan, invert the pan and plate together so that the tart transfers to the plate, with the pastry on the base. Serve hot or at room temperature with the whipped cheese.

VE Opt for vegan soft cheese, and olive oil for frying.
GF Use gluten-free pastry instead of the spelt pastry.

Broccoli Soup and Feta Cream

SERVES 4

olive oil, for frying

2 shallots, finely diced

3 garlic cloves, crushed

2 tablespoons lemon juice

1 litre vegetable stock

2 medium potatoes, peeled and finely
    diced

600g broccoli florets

a handful of fresh basil or mint

salt, to taste

pinch of freshly ground black pepper

FETA CREAM:

100g organic feta cheese, crumbled, or
    vegan yogurt mixed with 1 tablespoon
    nutritional yeast

100ml Greek or vegan yogurt

1 teaspoon honey or agave syrup

1 tablespoon extra virgin olive oil

This quick and easy soup has a good garlic hit balanced by tangy lemon, with the smooth and cooling feta and yogurt cream adding a contrasting highlight. Serve with freshly baked bread or salad.

Put all the ingredients for the feta cream in a blender or food processor and whizz until smooth. Set aside until ready to serve.

Heat a deep saucepan over a medium heat. Add a drizzle of olive oil and fry the shallots for 5–6 minutes, stirring. Stir in all the remaining ingredients and bring to the boil then reduce the heat and simmer for 10 minutes.

Transfer the soup to a blender or food processor and whizz until smooth, or blend in the pan with a hand-held blender. Serve with a drizzle of the feta cream.

Both the soup and the feta cream can be prepared 1–2 days in advance and kept, tightly covered or in an airtight container, in the fridge. Reheat the soup gently before serving.

VE Opt for vegan yogurt and nutritional yeast rather than feta cheese, vegan rather than Greek yogurt, and agave syrup.
GF Opt for tamari sauce; serve with gluten-free bread or omit the bread.

Courgette Involtini

SERVES 4/MAKES 12 ROLLS
500g ricotta or cottage cheese

2 garlic cloves, crushed

2 tablespoons lemon juice

½ teaspoon salt, or more to taste

¼ teaspoon freshly ground black pepper
    or a sprinkle of dried chilli flakes

olive oil, for drizzling

200ml Sugo Sauce or other tomato sauce
    (see page 143)

2 medium courgettes, each cut
    lengthways into 6 thin slices
    (12 slices in total)

100g cavolo nero (black cabbage or kale)
    stems removed and leaves
    finely chopped

grated Parmesan, rawmesan (see page
    28) or nutritional yeast for sprinkling

Italian cooking is wonderful for allowing ingredients to shine in their own right. Here, juicy courgette rolls are filled with a zesty, garlicky cheese mixture and cavolo nero, and baked on a thin layer of classic Italian tomato sauce to deliver lots of satisfying flavour. Delizioso! The courgette rolls also offer an ideal gluten-free alternative to pasta.

For a fresh herb take on this delicious dish, substitute basil or mixed tender summer herbs for the cavolo nero or add them, finely chopped, to the cheese mixture. To give the sugo sauce an extra dimension, blend in a roasted red pepper from a jar.

Preheat the oven to 200°C/gas mark 6. Mix together the cheese, garlic, lemon juice, salt and pepper or chilli flakes in a bowl. Drizzle olive oil over the base of a large ovenproof dish and pour in the sugo sauce.

To make the courgette rolls, lay a courgette slice on a work surface. Spread an even layer of the cheese mixture on top, then top with a thin layer of cavolo nero. Roll up and place in the sauce in the ovenproof dish. Repeat with the remainder of the courgette slices. Sprinkle the top with grated Parmesan, rawmesan or nutritional yeast and bake for 20–25 minutes. Serve hot or at room temperature. You can prepare the rolls a day ahead and keep, tightly covered, in the fridge.

VE Opt for vegan soft cheese or crème fraîche
and rawmesan or nutritional yeast.
GF ✓

Tip

You can alternatively make this dish using thinly sliced aubergines in place of courgettes. Just add a further 5–10 minutes to the baking time.

Mini Caesar Salad Baskets

SERVES 8

250g canned chickpeas (drained weight),
   rinsed and drained (optional)

2 avocados, chopped

8 large Cos (Romaine) lettuce leaves

VEGAN CAESAR DRESSING:

250ml vegan crème fraîche

2 tablespoons pine nuts

2 tablespoons nutritional yeast

2 tablespoons olive oil

1 tablespoon lemon juice

2 garlic cloves, peeled

1 teaspoon mustard

1 teaspoon drained capers

water, to thin the consistency

VEGETARIAN CAESAR DRESSING:

250ml crème fraîche

1 tablespoon pine nuts

2 tablespoons olive oil

1 tablespoon lemon juice

2 garlic cloves, peeled

1 teaspoon mustard

1 teaspoon drained capers

BASIC RAWMESAN:

2 tablespoons nutritional yeast

½ teaspoon salt

70g pine nuts or other nuts
   (walnuts are good)

1 garlic clove, minced

TOPPINGS:

grated Parmesan or rawmesan
   (see above)

pine nuts

capers

red onion, very thinly sliced

small croutons (I use sourdough) or
   panko breadcrumbs

Here, I've turned everyone's favourite salad into finger food! For this treat, use sturdy Cos (Romaine) lettuce leaves as edible bowls. My 'sort of Caesar' dressing comes in both fully vegan and vegetarian versions, which are equally delicious. Add the chickpeas for a more filling starter.

Put all the ingredients for the dressing of your choice in a blender and whizz to your desired consistency. Transfer to a bowl, cover tightly and refrigerate until ready to use. It will keep in the fridge for 3–4 days.

If using the chickpeas, heat a large frying pan over a medium-high heat, add the chickpeas and cook, tossing frequently, for about 5 minutes until crispy. Tip onto a plate and leave to cool.

In a bowl, mix the avocado with the chickpeas, if using, and half the dressing. If you want to make rawmesan, mix the ingredients together in a food processor.

Fill the lettuce leaves with the avocado mixture, then top with the Parmesan or rawmesan, pine nuts, capers, red onion and croutons or panko.

VE Use the vegan version of the Caesar dressing; opt for rawmesan for topping.
GF Use gluten-free croutons for topping.

Curried Flatbread Pizza

MAKES 6 PIZZAS
6 flatbreads of your choice

CURRY PASTE:
ghee or vegetable oil, for frying
3 shallots, thinly sliced
1½ tablespoons red wine vinegar
    or lemon juice
2 garlic cloves, crushed
1 tablespoon grated fresh ginger
½ red chilli, deseeded and finely
    chopped
1½ teaspoons ground turmeric
1 teaspoon ground cinnamon
    or cardamom
1½ teaspoons ground cumin
1 teaspoon thyme leaves
½ teaspoon salt, or more to taste
¼ teaspoon freshly ground black pepper
a handful of almonds, coarsely ground
250ml dairy or vegan yogurt
1 teaspoon honey or coconut sugar

SWEET GARLIC SAUCE:
150ml Greek yogurt
1 garlic clove, minced
½ teaspoon honey or agave syrup
pinch of salt

TOPPING OPTIONS:
cherry tomatoes, sliced
fresh coriander
baby spinach leaves
pickled red onion
piri piri peppers, finely chopped (for the
    hot spice lovers)
organic eggs

When time is in short supply but I want to make something really delicious for friends and family, I often throw together these Indian-style pizzas and they're always a hit! Don't be deterred by the list of ingredients, as the majority of them are spices you are likely to have already in your store cupboard.

The idea is to use ready-made flatbreads (keep a stock of them in the fridge, as I do). I like to use thin Turkish flatbreads, but Indian naan bread or Italian piadina flatbreads work just as well. Simply spread them with curry paste and bake them like a pizza, then serve them with fresh toppings. This is homemade fast food at its best! The pizzas can also be served whole for a more substantial meal.

Preheat the oven to 220°C/gas mark 7. To make the curry paste, heat a frying pan over a medium-high heat. Add a generous spoonful of ghee or a good drizzle of vegetable oil and fry the shallots, stirring frequently, for about 2 minutes until transparent. Add the vinegar or lemon juice, garlic, spices, thyme, salt and pepper and cook, stirring, for 2–3 minutes. Add the almonds and more ghee or vegetable oil if needed and fry, stirring frequently, for about 1–2 minutes until the almonds are toasted. Reduce the heat, add the yogurt with the honey or coconut sugar and cook, stirring constantly, for 2–3 minutes. Turn off the heat.

Mix together the ingredients for the sweet garlic sauce in a small bowl and set aside until ready to serve.

Lay the flatbreads on a large baking tray and spread with the curry paste. Bake for 30 seconds–2 minutes, depending on the thickness of the breads, keeping an eye on the breads to avoid them burning – if they are thin, they can quickly catch. I bake in batches of 1–2 breads at a time. Remove from the oven, scatter with your choice of toppings and drizzle with the garlic sauce. Cut into slices for sharing.

The curry paste can be made 3–4 days in advance – leave to cool, transfer to an airtight container and keep in the fridge.

Tip
Crack an egg over each flatbread before baking in the oven.

VE Opt for vegetable oil and coconut sugar for the curry paste; vegan yogurt and agave syrup for the sauce; don't use eggs as a topping.
GF Use gluten-free flatbreads, such as corn tortillas.

Pink Grapefruit Margarita

A cocktail with lively citrus will open your get-together with zest! I use pink grapefruit for its beautiful colour, but you can use any citrus you like. With its Mexican origins, this drink is a natural match for tacos and other Latin flavours.

SERVES 1
40ml fresh pink grapefruit juice
40ml tequila
1 tablespoon agave syrup
1 tablespoon fresh lime juice
ice cubes

SALTED HOT LIME RIM:
coarse sea salt
2 tablespoons water
1 tablespoon fresh lime juice
sprinkle of ground chilli

TO SERVE:
crushed ice
½ lime wheel

First prepare the salted hot lime rim. Make a layer of salt on a saucer or small plate. Mix together the water and lime juice in a shallow bowl. Dip the rim of a cocktail glass in the liquid to moisten it and then dip the rim in the salt.

Put the pink grapefruit juice, tequila, agave syrup and lime juice in a mixing glass with a few ice cubes and stir together well.

Add some crushed ice to a glass, then pour the cocktail through a sieve into the glass, add the lime wheel half and serve.

Tip. *Simply omit the tequila for a zesty mocktail.*

VE ✓ GF ✓

Mango Lassi

Refreshening and alcohol free, a smooth mango lassi will also chill down the heat of a spicy curry, or cool you down on a hot summer's day. Lassi is a yogurt-based drink popular in India and surrounding countries and can be either savoury or sweet. The most popular version of lassi worldwide is mango, which contains no added sugar, sweetened only by fresh mango pulp.

SERVES 2
1 ripe mango, chopped
grated zest of 1 lime
½ teaspoon fresh lime juice
500ml yogurt, preferable coconut
pinch of ground cardamom (optional)
ice cubes

Put all the ingredients except the ice cubes in a blender and whizz until smooth. Add some ice cubes to two glasses, pour over the mango lassi and serve.

VE Opt for vegan yogurt.
GF ✓

Tip *Serve in cocktail glasses for a fruity mocktail.*

Golden Milk Latte

Serving your guests this golden latte will make them feel extra nourished and cherished. Haldi ka doodh, or golden milk as it's more often called in the Western world, is an Ayurvedic turmeric-flavoured warm milk drink that has been enjoyed in India since ancient times. Golden milk is now making a splash outside of India, too, with a few tweaks to make it extra appealing to our Westernised palates. This version is sweetened with honey or agave syrup and has a touch of comforting cinnamon added.

SERVES 1
1 tablespoon finely grated fresh turmeric or ground turmeric
1 teaspoon honey or agave syrup
1 teaspoon finely grated fresh ginger
½ teaspoon fresh lemon juice
pinch of ground cardamom
pinch of ground cinnamon
pinch of freshly ground black pepper
250ml dairy or plant-based milk of your choice

Put all the ingredients, except the milk, in a blender and whizz to a smooth paste.

Bring the milk to a simmer in a saucepan, pour into the blender and whizz until combined. Serve in a glass or cup.

VE Opt for agave syrup and a plant-based milk.
GF ✓

Rainbow Crudités with Artichoke Dip

Nothing shouts out feast more than a platter full to the brim with ripe vegetables in the colours of the rainbow! Choose quality ingredients and take care in cutting the vegetables into handy sizes and tempting shapes. The key to a successful veggie platter is to team up the crudités with a delicious savoury dip.

The artichoke cream, made from the hearts of globe artichokes and flavoured with mustard and capers, is just that and this one is enhanced by fresh dill, plus a little yogurt for creamy perfection. The dip can be prepared a day ahead and the vegetables can be prepared on the same day and will keep fresh, if sealed, in the fridge, for a few hours.

SERVES 6

1.2kg fresh raw vegetables, such as cucumber, radishes, cauliflower, peppers, cherry tomatoes, carrots and/or beetroot

ARTICHOKE DIP

300g jarred or canned artichoke hearts, drained
3 tablespoons crème fraîche
2 tablespoons finely chopped dill
1 garlic clove, crushed
1 teaspoon drained capers
50ml olive oil
1 tablespoon Dijon mustard
1 teaspoon honey or agave syrup
salt and freshly ground black pepper, to taste

Peel and trim the vegetables as necessary, then cut them into manageable and attractive sizes and shapes.

For the artichoke dip, mix the ingredients in a food processor until a smooth cream is formed. To serve, arrange the vegetables and dip on a platter.

VE Opt for vegan crème fraîche and agave syrup instead of honey.
GF ✓

Classic Hummus

Hummus is maybe one of the world's most popular dips. And for good reason: it's incredibly delicious! This recipe is based on classic hummus using a little yogurt for extra silky creaminess. You can vary the hummus by adding fresh herbs like coriander, and veggies such as cooked squash or beets. Hummus can be prepared a day in advance and kept, tightly covered or in an airtight container, in the fridge. Serve with crudités or bread and swirl in some spicy harissa if you like a hot kick to it.

SERVES 4

2 garlic cloves, peeled
50ml water
2 x 400g cans chickpeas, drained
3 tablespoons tahini
2 tablespoons yogurt (optional)
1½ tablespoons lemon juice
salt, to taste

TO SERVE

1 teaspoon harisa, for serving (optional)

Blend all the ingredients until smooth, adding small amounts of water until it is at the desired consistency.

VE Use vegan yogurt
GF ✓

Smoky Sweet Potato Tahini Pie

SERVES 4

SPELT PASTRY:
180g spelt flour
¼ teaspoon salt
125g butter, chilled, or coconut oil,
    soft but not liquid
about 2 tablespoons cold water

SWEET POTATO FILLING:
5-6 medium sweet potatoes
olive oil, for drizzling
1½ teaspoons dried thyme
100g Parmesan, finely grated
100g ricotta
2 tablespoons tahini
1½ teaspoons lemon juice
1 teaspoon honey or agave syrup
¾ tablespoon smoked paprika

a handful of caramelised almonds or
    pecans, to garnish
salt and freshly ground black pepper,
    to taste

When you want a comforting meal to share, a savoury pie is sure to delight everyone around the table. This pie features a simple spelt pastry case, filled with creamy ricotta and sweet potato combined with tahini and smoked paprika, and topped with caramelised almonds, so there's plenty of flavour and texture at play here. Serve in slices with a tangy green salad.

Preheat the oven to 220°C/gas mark 7. Line a baking tray with baking paper.

To make the pastry, mix together the flour and salt in a bowl. Add the butter or coconut oil in small pieces and rub it into the flour with your fingertips or work it in with a fork until evenly combined and the texture resembles breadcrumbs. Mix in the cold water to form a dough. Wrap in clingfilm and leave to rest in the fridge for 30 minutes.

While the pastry is resting, start preparing the filling. Peel the sweet potatoes. Slice ten thin rounds from one sweet potato for the topping and reserve. Chop the remaining sweet potato into large dice (about 2cm pieces) and put in a bowl. Drizzle with olive oil and toss to coat evenly, then sprinkle with the thyme and season with salt and pepper. Spread out on the lined baking tray and bake for 15-20 minutes, keeping watch on them to avoid burning. Remove from the oven and lower the oven temperature to 180°C/ gas mark 4.

Roll out the pastry and press into a large (about 20-23cm diameter) pie dish to line the base and sides, then bake for 10 minutes. Meanwhile, put the roasted sweet potato in a food processor with all the remaining filling ingredients and whizz to a smooth purée.

Tip the filling into the pastry case and arrange the reserved rounds of sweet potato on top. Bake for a further 30 minutes until browned on top. Sprinkle with the caramelised almonds and serve at room temperature.

The pastry can be made 2-3 days in advance and stored, wrapped, in the fridge. The pie can be prepared a day ahead of serving and kept, covered, in the fridge.

VE Opt for coconut oil for the pastry; rawmesan,
vegan soft cheese and agave syrup for the filling.
GF Use gluten-free pastry instead of the spelt pastry.

2. MIDSUMMER FEAST

In Scandivania, around the time of the summer solstice, midsummer feasts are held throughout the day and long light nights. These feasts are often staged alfresco with the table adorned with freshly picked flowers, which guests also use to decorate their hair.

The food is a celebration of characteristic Nordic flavours, in particular fresh herbs and preserves, and a smörgåsbord – a wide variety of dishes – is the most popular form for the meal. But sometimes, all those flavours are gathered together in one dish, known as smörgåstårta – a savoury sandwich cake.

Midsummer would not be complete without everyone enjoying a luscious strawberry sponge cake to round off the feast, before dancing barefoot and skinny-dipping late into the evening in a nearby lake or the sea. This chapter contains all the recipes you need to create your own Scandi-style summer feast.

Green Pea and Broccoli Fritters

MAKES 12 FRITTERS

DILL AND HORSERADISH CREAM:
200ml Greek yogurt
2 tablespoons finely chopped dill
1 garlic clove, minced
1 tablespoon extra virgin olive oil
1 teaspoon horseradish paste, or
    ½ teaspoon wasabi paste
½ teaspoon honey or agave syrup
½ teaspoon lemon juice
salt and freshly ground black pepper,
    to taste

FRITTERS:
200g broccoli, chopped
100g grated Parmesan or rawmesan
    (see page 28)
200g fresh or frozen peas
1 medium organic egg, lightly beaten
70g panko (optional)
½ teaspoon salt
¼ teaspoon freshly ground black pepper
vegetable oil, for frying

red onion, sliced or chopped, to serve
with the dill and horesradish cream

Green peas and broccoli are bound together in these delicious Nordic style falafels. Serve them as appetisers or as part of the smörgåsbord, or in a pitta bread with salad as Scandinavian version of falafel bread.

The contrastingly cool yogurt sauce is enhanced with horseradish and dill, flavourings that classically define Scandinavian cooking and are regarded as the Nordic equivalent of chilli and garlic. You can substitute the horseradish with wasabi paste for an interesting twist.

———

Mix together all the ingredients for the dill and horseradish cream in a bowl, then cover tightly and refrigerate until ready to serve. It can be made a day in advance and kept in the fridge.

Preheat the oven to 110°C/gas mark ¼. Line a baking tray with baking paper. Mix the fritter ingredients together in a food processor. Taste and adjust with salt and pepper. Heat a frying pan to a medium-high heat. Add a drizzle of vegetable oil. Scoop up 1 tablespoon of fritter mixture per ball and fry the fritters in batches, for about 4–5 minutes turning carefully to fry all sides. Transfer each fried fritter to the lined tray and keep hot in the oven while you finish frying the remainder.

Once all fried, serve the fritters with the dill and horseradish cream.

VE Opt for vegan yogurt, agave syrup, rawmesan and omit the egg or use a vegan egg replacer.
GF Opt for gluten-free breadcrumbs.

Smörgåsbord

SERVES 6

NEW POTATOES WITH DILL AND CHIVES:
1.2kg new potatoes, lightly scrubbed
pinch of salt, plus extra to taste
a handful of roughly chopped dill
15g butter or a drizzle of olive oil
a handful of finely chopped chives

PICKLED VEG:
100ml cider vinegar
1 tablespoon sugar or agave syrup
1 teaspoon salt, plus an extra pinch
    to season the sauce
200g prepared mixed vegetables of your
    choice, such as red onion, carrots,
    beetroot, cucumber, courgette, roasted
    cauliflower florets and cabbage, peeled
    where appropriate and thinly sliced
    or chopped

MUSTARD SOURED CREAM SAUCE:
150ml soured cream or vegan crème
    fraîche
1 tablespoon Dijon mustard
1 teaspoon honey or agave syrup

Herbed Lentil Meatballs (see page 56)

OTHER SMÖRGÅSBORD ADDITIONS:
5 medium organic eggs, boiled for 8–10
    minutes, drained and cooled in cold
    water and peeled
Smoked Tofu Rillette (see page 44)
red onion, finely chopped
knäckebröd or crisp crackers and breads
butter
cheese

The Swedish *smörgåsbord* dates back to the 16th century and traditionally consists of a whole table of Scandinavian delicacies served cold and warm, and it remains today how Swedes enjoy holiday food. While all the dishes in this chapter are designed to work perfectly as part of a smörgåsbord, these are the all-important additions that complete the smörgåsbord experience. Pickles are always great for topping all sorts of savoury food and Scandinavian pickles are no exception. These mixed pickled veg in a creamy mustard sauce make the perfect vegetarian alternative to Swedish pickled herring – delicious served with boiled new potatoes with fresh herbs, hard-boiled eggs (or marinated tofu) and *knäckebröd* (Swedish crispbread), or other rustic bread like sourdough (as seen here) or rye bread.

———

To prepare the new potatoes with dill and chives, put the potatoes in a saucepan and cover generously with water. Add the salt and dill, bring to the boil and cook until the potatoes are tender – about 10–20 minutes, depending on the size of the potatoes. Drain the cooked potatoes and put in a bowl. Add the butter or olive oil, sprinkle with salt to taste and toss with the chives.

To prepare the pickled veg, mix together the vinegar, sugar or agave syrup and salt in a glass jug. Pack the prepared vegetables of your choice into a sterilised jar and pour over the pickling liquid. Seal the jar and leave to soak for an hour before serving. The pickled veg will keep, in the sealed jar, in the fridge for 10–14 days.

When ready to serve, mix together the soured cream, mustard and a pinch of salt in a bowl. Drain the pickled veg and serve.

VE Opt for olive oil and vegan soured cream,
butter and cheese.
GF Use gluten-free crispbreads or crackers
and breads.

Smoked Tofu Rillette

This sumptuous spread combining smoked tofu, garlic and nutritional yeast brings a powerful, typically Scandinavian umami savour to breads, crackers and Smörgåstårta (see page 47). Slightly smoky, almost fishy in flavour with a rich creaminess, I use it as a faux mackerel spread on bread with pickles and fresh toppings. I've included a few optional variations in the ingredients, which are all equally delicious.

SERVES 4–6/MAKES ABOUT 500G
350g smoked tofu
100g mayonnaise
2 tablespoons shoyu soy or tamari sauce
1 tablespoon nutritional yeast or grated Parmesan
1 garlic clove, minced
1 tablespoon extra virgin olive oil
salt and freshly ground black pepper, to taste

OPTIONAL ADDITIONS/VARIATIONS
   (CHOOSE ONE OR TWO):
2 tablespoons finely shredded ready-toasted nori
1 tablespoon finely chopped tarragon or dill
1 tablespoon finely chopped dragon fruit flesh
1 teaspoon lemon juice
substitute 1 tablespoon toasted sesame oil for the extra
   virgin olive oil

Lightly press the smoked tofu between sheets of kitchen paper and leave for a few minutes to absorb the excess moisture.

Put all the ingredients in a blender or food processor and whizz to a smooth cream. The rillette will keep, in an airtight container, in the fridge for 4–5 days.

VE Opt for vegan mayonnaise and nutritional yeast.
GF Opt for tamari sauce and gluten-free mayonnaise.

Green Garden Salad

This vibrant green salad combines lightly fried fresh asparagus and spring onions with baby spinach, dressed with a zesty lemon and mustard dressing, to make the perfect side for Nordic dishes. Try substituting green beans or tenderstem broccoli for the asparagus to make this salad at other times of the year.

SERVES 4
a handful of medium asparagus spears
olive oil, for frying
4 spring onions, thinly sliced
a handful of baby spinach
240g butter beans, rinsed and drained
4 medium organic eggs, boiled for 8–10 minutes,
   drained and cooled in cold water and peeled
1 avocado, thinly sliced
salt and freshly ground black pepper, to taste

LEMON AND MUSTARD DRESSING:
1 tablespoon extra virgin olive oil
1 tablespoon lemon juice
½ tablespoon Dijon mustard
½ teaspoon honey or agave syrup

Whisk together the ingredients for the lemon and mustard dressing in a small bowl until well blended and set aside.

Snap or cut off the woody ends of the asparagus spears. Heat a wide frying pan over a medium-high heat. Add a drizzle of olive oil and fry the asparagus and spring onions for about 3 minutes, turning frequently. Add the lemon juice and season to taste with salt and pepper.

Arrange the asparagus and spring onions with the baby spinach and butter beans on a serving plate. Grate or crumble over the egg, add the avocado and sprinkle with the capers. Season lightly with salt and pepper and drizzle with the dressing.

VE Use 200g crumbled smoked tofu instead of eggs.
Opt for agave syrup for the dressing.
GF ✓

Seaweed caviar

Seaweed caviar is the brilliant invention of molecular gastronomy, an experimental and scientific style of cooking. By transforming liquified seaweed into tiny pearls, the flavour and texture of caviar is achieved. Seaweed caviar is increasingly popular due to its delicious flavour, as caviar for vegetarians and vegans. As a food product, it is a far more eco-conscious choice than fish caviar. You will find it in fine food stores and online.

Smörgåstårta

SERVES 6

LAYER 1:
    Smoked Tofu Rillette (see page 44)

LAYER 2 – NORDIC EGG SALAD:
5 medium organic eggs, boiled for 8–10
    minutes, drained and cooled in cold
    water and peeled
150ml crème fraîche
5 tablespoons finely chopped chives
3 tablespoons finely chopped dill
1 tablespoon grated lemon zest
1 tablespoon Dijon mustard
salt and freshly ground black pepper,
    to taste

LAYER 3 – AVOCADO:
mayonnaise, for spreading
4 avocados, thinly sliced (reserve a few
    slices to decorate)
squeeze of lemon juice

TO ASSEMBLE:
4 long slices of spelt or wheat bread, or
    gluten-free bread, crusts trimmed
150g mascarpone or crème fraîche

TO DECORATE:
a handful of fine sprouts, such as radish
    sprouts, alfalfa or betroot sprouts, and/
    or microgreens of your choice
½ red onion, pickled or finely chopped
2–3 radishes, thinly sliced
4–6 cucumber ribbons
2 tablespoons seaweed caviar (optional)

Tip
*Ask your baker to slice the loaf of your
choice horizontally, then all you need to
do is trim the crusts. You can also piece
together squares of pre-sliced sandwich
bread – just trim the crusts and make sure
that the slices are the same size.*

**This over-the-top sandwich cake holds the number one spot in
Sweden for party food at milestone celebrations, such as birthdays
and graduation parties. With the rising interest in Nordic food culture,
smörgåstårta has gained an elevated status in recent times and you can
now often find versions of this once folksy cake in refined restaurants.
Traditionally made with prawns, salmon or ham, my version replicates
all the characteristic flavours of the original using my delicious Smoked
Tofu Rillette (see page 44), egg salad and avocado. The ingredients for
decorating the cake can be varied according to the season, or make your
own creative choices. Make the cake entirely vegan by substituting the
egg salad for the Artichoke Dip (see page 34) or your bean dip of choice.**

Mix together all the ingredients for the Nordic egg salad in a bowl. You can
prepare this a day ahead and store, tightly covered, in the fridge.

To assemble the cake, lay a sheet of baking paper on a tray or wooden
board. Place a slice of bread on the paper and spread with an even layer of
the smoked tofu rillette. Top with another slice of bread. Spread the second
layer with an even layer of the egg salad. Add a third slice of bread and spread
with a thin layer of mayonnaise, then arrange the avocado slices on top in an
even layer and squeeze over a little lemon juice. Add the fourth slice of bread.
Spread the mascarpone or crème fraîche over the top and sides of the cake.
Decorate with the ingredients listed and serve as soon as possible.

VE Opt for vegan crème fraîche and mayonnaise. Use
Artichoke Dip (see page 34) or vegan bean spread.
GF Use gluten-free bread and mayonnaise.

Tip
To achieve the appropriate flavour without using Västerbotten cheese, use a 50:50 mixture of aged mature Cheddar and Parmesan.

Västerbotten Pies

MAKES/SERVES 6
1 quantity of Spelt Pastry (see page 22)
300g prepared vegetables, such as
  broccoli or spinach, tomatoes,
  potatoes or leeks

FILLING:
250g Västerbotten cheese or other sharp
  nutty dairy cheese (or see the Tip), or
  vegan hard cheese, grated
3 medium organic eggs
100ml single dairy cream or full-fat
  Greek yogurt
100ml dairy or plant-based milk of
  your choice
3 bird's eye red chilli peppers, drained
  and deseeded except for a few seeds,
  then pounded to a paste using a pestle
  and mortar (optional)
pinch each of salt and freshly ground
  black pepper

TOPPINGS:
red onion
yogurt
tomatoes

The indulgent rich and creamy filling of these pies is made with Västerbotten cheese, an aged Swedish cheese with a pronounced flavour reminiscent of a mixture of Parmesan and Cheddar. Here, I've taken the traditional recipe further by adding vegetables to the filling because, as we all know, cheese and veggies are a match made in heaven. I've also added a bit of heat to the pies, using sharp piri piri, inspired by my artist friend Adelaster, who served a chilli-hot version of Västerbotten pie when I visited her in Sweden. Traditionally, this pie uses dairy cheese and cream, but the filling can easily be made with plant-based ingredients – try using blended silken tofu or dairy-free cooking cream, or cashew cream, instead of cheese and single cream, and add vegan cheese or 75g nutritional yeast and adjust the taste with salt, pepper and olive oil.

Preheat the oven to 220°C/gas mark 7. Prepare the vegetables by boiling scrubbed or peeled potatoes for up to 20 minutes or until soft in the middle. Drain and slice thinly. If using a whole broccoli, cut into florets and steam for four minutes before cutting into smaller pieces. If using leeks, cut them into thin slices.

Press the pastry into six tartlet tins (6–7cm diameter) or one large flan/quiche tin (24cm diameter) to line the base sides, then bake for 10 minutes. Meanwhile, put all the ingredients for the filling in a blender or food processor and whizz until smooth.

Pour the filling into the pastry cases or case and add your chosen prepared vegetables, distributing them evenly. Bake for a further 12–15 minutes for the small pies and 20 minutes for the large pie. Leave to cool before serving.

The cooked pies can be prepared up to two days before serving and stored, covered, in the fridge.

VE Opt for coconut oil for the pastry; vegan cheese, vegan yogurt, vegan egg replacer, vegan cooking cream and plant-based milk for the filling.
GF Used gluten-free pastry.

Midsummer Dream Cake

SERVES 8

SPONGE CAKE
250g spelt flour
75g raw cacao powder or cocoa powder
2 teaspoons baking powder
⅔ teaspoon fine salt
½ teaspoon ground cardamom
125g coconut oil or butter, plus extra
    for greasing
1 banana, mashed to a smooth purée
160ml plant-based or dairy milk
grated zest of ½ orange
50ml mango or fresh orange juice
2 teaspoon vanilla extract
125g honey or agave syrup

RASPBERRY FILLING:
200g mascarpone or crème fraîche
1 teaspoon fresh lemon juice
75g raspberries, fresh or frozen
2 tablespoons honey or agave syrup

MASCARPONE ICING:
200g mascarpone or crème fraîche
3 tablespoons honey or agave syrup
1 teaspoon fresh lemon juice
½ teaspoon vanilla extract
pinch of salt
ground cinnamon, for dusting

DECORATION
300g strawberries, halved
other berries and fresh wild flowers
    (optional)

Most Swedes would agree that Midsummer wouldn't be the same without a proper strawberry sponge cake. Swedish sponge cakes are often made extra juicy by the addition of fruit juice, and in this case I've chosen to use mango and orange juice, along with a touch of cardamom for extra aromatic interest. I wanted to devise a sponge cake recipe without using eggs, so I've added mashed banana instead. That and the use of spelt flour, which I really like in baking for its nutty flavour, makes the sponge a little denser and moister than the traditional kind. It's also easy to substitute plant-based ingredients for the dairy items in the filling and frosting as suggested.

To decorate, use a few common edible wild flowers if you have the opportunity to pick them – after all, Midsummer is all about celebrating the great outdoors in full bloom!

———

Preheat the oven to 180°C/gas mark 4 and grease a 20cm springform tin with coconut oil. Put the dry ingredients in a mixing bowl and mix well together. Melt the coconut oil or butter slowly in a pan. Put the honey, milk, orange zest, juice, mashed banana and vanilla extract in a second bowl and add the melted oil or butter. Whisk the wet ingredients together, either by hand or using an electric mixer.

Pour the wet mixture into the bowl with the dry ingredients and mix well. Pour the batter into the greased tin and level the surface using a spatula or the back of a spoon. Bake for 1 hour. Test by inserting a skewer into the centre: if it comes out dry and clean, the cake is cooked. Bake for a few minutes longer if it needs it. Remove from the oven and allow the cake to rest and cool.

To make the raspberry filling, mix all the ingredients together. Set aside in the fridge. To make the mascarpone icing, briskly whip the ingredients together. Set aside in the fridge until ready to assemble the cake.

When the cake is cool, halve it horizontally and gently lift off the top half and set aside carefully. Add a generous layer of raspberry filling to the cake base then place the top half on the filling. Carefully spread a thick even layer of the mascarpone icing over the top of the cake.

Decorate the assembled cake with halved strawberries. It looks beautiful and festive to arrange flowers and berries around the base or on top with the strawberries.

VE Use coconut oil or olive oil instead of butter; opt for agave syrup instead of honey; and use vegan crème fraîche instead of mascarpone and cottage cheese.
GF This cake is not gluten-free.

3. MIDWINTER FEAST

A variety of comforting dishes is what's needed to create a warm, welcoming Midwinter table, and in this chapter, colourful beetroots and greens are used to create a feast for the eye as well as the taste buds. But it wouldn't be complete without a centrepiece roast, so here you'll also find a whole thyme and garlic-roasted cauliflower and mustard-and-miso-rubbed celeriac served sliced into steaks. To contrast and complement, there are fresh, sweet and tangy sides featuring cabbage, onion and citrus, and roots roasts, while a delicious gravy adds a luxurious enriching element to that Swedish essential – meatballs – here reinterpreted with lentils and herbs. And for a show-stopping finish, there is an impressive chocolate cake with deep, dark flavours from dates and beetroot.
Winter never tasted so good!

Warm Mulled Apple Juice

Mulled warm drinks, especially spiced wines, are essential during the festive winter season in northern Europe. This alchol-free mulled apple juice is both refreshing and warming, the spices add a beautiful flavour and best of all it can be shared with everyone, from children to designated drivers.

MAKES 2 LITRES
2 litres good-quality unsweetened apple juice
2 tablespoons honey or agave syrup
5 cloves
2 cinnamon sticks, plus extra to serve
4 star anise, plus extra to serve
slices of citrus fruit, plus extra to serve

Put all the ingredients, except the extras for serving, in a large saucepan that has a lid. Bring to the boil, then reduce the heat, cover the pan with the lid and simmer for 30 minutes.

To serve, ladle into cups or handled glasses and add an extra star anise, a citrus slice and a cinnamon stick to each.

VE Opt for agave syrup.
GF ✓

Blackberry Onion Confit

The natural sweetness of the red onions is intensified in this jam-like condiment, which acts well as a counterbalance to intensely savoury dishes. It's delicious served with root vegetables. The optional puréed blackberries can be substituted with other berries or fruit, such as cranberries, blueberries, cloudberries and figs.

MAKES ABOUT 300G
olive oil or unsalted butter, for frying
3 medium red onions, thinly sliced
4 tablespoons coconut sugar or agave syrup
4 tablespoons red wine vinegar
2 tablespoons puréed blackberries
pinch of salt

Heat a frying pan over a medium heat. Add a drizzle of olive oil or a little butter and fry the onions for about 10–12 minutes, stirring, until soft and just translucent. Add the remaining ingredients and cook over a low heat, stirring, for 10 minutes until the liquid has reduced. Transfer to a sterilised jar, seal and leave to cool.

The confit can be stored in the fridge for up to 5 days. Leave at room temperature for an hour before serving.

VE Opt for olive oil.
GF ✓

Herbed Lentil Meatballs with Green Peppercorn Gravy

SERVES 6/MAKES 32 BALLS

HERBED LENTIL MEATBALLS:

800g cooked Puy or green lentils
4 tablespoons finely chopped
    thyme leaves
140g onion, finely chopped and sautéed
160g panko breadcrumbs or cooked
    brown rice
4 garlic cloves, crushed
4 tablespoons nutritional yeast or
    grated Parmesan
2 teaspoons salt, plus extra to taste
½ teaspoon freshly ground black
    pepper, plus extra to taste
1 tablespoon mustard
2 generous handfuls of delicate herbs,
    such as basil and flat-leaf parsley,
    finely chopped
1 teaspoon honey or agave syrup
olive oil or ghee or butter, for frying

GREEN PEPPERCORN GRAVY:

2 tablespoons ghee, butter or
    vegetable oil
2 tablespoons drained green
    peppercorns in brine
2 tablespoons apple purée
150ml vegetable stock
3 tablespoons shoyu soy or tamari sauce
150ml double cream
salt, to taste
1 tablespoon kuzu or rice flour or
    plain flour, for thickening (optional)

As with the Midsummer Feast (see page 39), the Swedish Christmas table is a smörgåsbord of savoury dishes, along with pickles and slightly sweet sides, and typically Swedish meatballs. Here I've adapted my 'neatballs' recipe from *Bowls of Goodness*, using cooked lentils and fresh fragrant herbs, perfectly complemented by a piquant green peppercorn gravy, making a delicous Midwinter Feast dish. Serve with the Blackberry Onion Confit (see page 55) and Gratin Dauphinois (see page 58) or puffed potatoes (see page 65), or mash.

To prepare the meatballs, mix together all the ingredients in a bowl, then transfer to a food processor and pulse for a few seconds until coarsely ground – be careful not to over-process or the mixture will become too smooth. Return the mixture to the bowl, cover and leave to rest in the fridge for 30 minutes.

Preheat the oven to 110°C/gas mark ¼. Line a baking tray with baking paper. Wet your hands, or oil them, and form the mixture into small balls about 2.5cm in diameter. Heat a frying pan over a medium-high heat. Add a drizzle of olive oil, a little ghee or butter and fry the balls, in batches, for 2–3 minutes. Transfer the fried balls to the lined tray and keep warm while you finish frying all the balls and are ready to serve.

Meanwhile, to make the green peppercorn gravy, heat a saucepan over a medium-high heat. Add the ghee, butter or vegetable oil, and once hot, add all the remaining ingredients except the thickener and whisk the gravy until it's smooth and hot. Taste and adjust the seasoning with salt. If you want to thicken the gravy, crush the kuzu pieces using a pestle and mortar, then dissolve it in 2 tablespoons of cold water, add to the sauce and whisk until combined and smooth. If you are using rice flour or plain flour, mix with 1 tablespoon of cold water to a smooth paste, then whisk into the gravy. Simmer for a couple of minutes until thickened. Serve the warm herbed lentil meatballs with the green peppercorn gravy.

Tip
Add 1 tablespoon of Cognac to the sauce for extra flavour interest, unless serving to children.

VE Opt for olive oil for frying; nutritional yeast and agave syrup for the meatballs; vegetable oil and vegan cooking cream for the gravy.
GF Opt for cooked brown rice or use gluten-free breadcrumbs instead of panko for the meatballs; tamari sauce for the gravy.

Gratin Dauphinois with Roasted Leeks

Gratin Dauphinois will have great sentimental value for those who, like me, grew up in the seventies and eighties, as it was the go-to festive potato dish. For everyone else, it's just an incredibly tasty, classic French dish. Covering thin slices of potato in a garlicy creamy sauce is just brilliant and it works decade after decade! This decadent gratin can be custom-made to suit everyone: read the extra note on cooking cream and milk below.

SERVES 6

1kg waxy potatoes, scrubbed, and thinly sliced on a mandolin or with a knife
2 garlic cloves, minced
2 shallots, thinly sliced
250ml cooking cream of choice, see note
250ml plant-based or dairy milk
1¼ teaspoons salt
½ teaspoon freshly ground black pepper
2 teaspoons thyme leaves, plus extra for sprinkling
2 small baby leeks or 4 spring onions, ends trimmed off and halved lengthways
100g rawmesan (see page 28), Parmesan or other cheese of choice
a drizzle of olive oil

Preheat the oven to 160°C/gas mark 3. Grease the inside of a large oven-proof dish and arrange the potato slices in overlapping layers. Combine the garlic, shallots, cream, milk, salt, pepper and thyme in a saucepan. Bring to the boil and then lower the temperature to simmer. Stir and simmer for 5 minutes. Pour over the potatoes.

Brush the leeks with olive oil and press them down into the gratin. Bake for 50–60 minutes, keeping an eye on them in the last 10 minutes to avoid burning. Sprinkle with cheese and bake for a further 10 minutes. Serve warm with other dishes such as the lentil meatballs (see page 56) or roasted cauliflower (see page 61).

VE Opt for plant-based milk, vegan cooking cream and rawmesan.
GF ✓

Cream of the crop!
Many classic French dishes and 'old-school' cooking in general can be heavy on dairy cream, butter and cheese, and if you are looking to decrease your intake of animal protein there's many good options for replacing dairy.

The good news is that you can enjoy it all, with some tweaks, wherever a recipe calls for butter, use olive oil instead. Natural food stores are stocking more plant-based cooking creams as the vegan diet is becoming increasingly popular. Diluted nut butters and coconut milk, cashew cream and silky tofu all make good alternatives to dairy cream.

Cauliflower Roast

Cauliflower is a champion in the kitchen, making delicious roasts as well as mashes and sauces. This roast uses a simple rub of garlicky olive oil, finished with nutritional yeast or Parmesan and lemon juice, allowing the natural flavour of the cauli to shine.

SERVES 6 (AS A SIDE)
100ml olive oil, plus extra if needed
2 garlic cloves, crushed
1 large cauliflower, about 1kg, leaves removed
    and stalk trimmed
4–5 thyme sprigs
40g nutritional yeast or Parmesan, grated
juice of 1 lemon
1 tablespoon agave syrup
salt and freshly ground black pepper, to taste

CASHEW TAHINI SAUCE:
1 tablespoon tahini
1 tablespoon shoyu soy or tamari
75g pre-soaked cashew nuts, drained
1 tablespoon olive oil
1½ tablespoons lemon juice
1 garlic clove, crushed
1 teaspoon agave syrup or honey
½ teaspoon salt and more, to taste
water, to thin

Preheat the oven to 220°C/gas mark 7. Mix together half the olive oil and all the garlic in a small bowl. Drizzle some over the cauliflower on a baking tray. Turn the cauliflower upside down and lightly drizzle or spray the inside with the rest of the garlicky olive oil. Insert thyme sprigs into cavities of the cauli, then sprinkle with salt and pepper. Roast for 1 hour.

When the cauli is roasting, blend the cashew tahini sauce together until smooth. Add small amounts of water until desired consistency.

Remove from the oven and leave to cool slightly. Meanwhile, mix the remainder of the olive oil with the nutritional yeast or Parmesan, lemon juice and agave syrup in a small bowl. Drizzle over and then rub into the roasted cauli. Roast for a further 5 minutes. Transfer the cauli whole to a serving platter, then slice to serve.

VE Opt for nutritional yeast.
GF ✓

Tip
You can easily vary the seasoning rub for the cauliflower by using tikka masala or harissa and tahini blended with olive oil and salt or vegetarian or vegan pesto.

Winter Coleslaw

In the winter, cabbage often replaces more tender green leaves in my salads. This vibrant coleslaw adds a fresh contrast to fried and roasted dishes.

SERVES 6
½ head white cabbage, finely shredded
½ head red cabbage, finely shredded
½ red onion, thinly sliced
2 carrots, julienned
a small handful of fresh mint, parsley or coriander,
    thinly sliced
50g walnuts, crumbled

MUSTARD MAYONNAISE
1 tablespoon Dijon mustard
1 teaspoon apple cider vinegar
50ml mayonnaise or vegan mayonnaise
juice of ½ lemon (about 1 tablespoon)
½ teaspoon salt, plus extra to taste
1 teaspoon olive oil

Mix the mayonnaise ingredients together in a small bowl. Toss the remaining ingredients in a serving bowl. Pour the mayo over and toss to combine.

VE Opt for vegan mayonnaise.
GF Opt for gluten-free mayonnaise.

From top left:
Chai Carrot Cake,
page 186. Mini Caesar
Salad Baskets, page 28.
Lemongrass and Butternut
Soup, page 139. Seared
Brussels Sprouts with
Pomegranate, page 64.
Best Tomato Salad Ever
(with spinach and avocado
and sourdough croutons
added), page 138.
Roasted Baby Pumpkins
Stuffed with Harissa
Lentils, page 115.
Cauliflower Roast, page
61. Winter Coleslaw,
page 61.
Green Pancakes, from
the Green Crêpe Cake,
page 154.

Citrus Salad

A zingy citrus salad brightens up winter dinners and delivers a dose of vitamin D as a bonus. And it doesn't need much to shine – a simple vinaigrette and fresh herbs will do the trick. Include the spinach and nuts to make a more substantial side dish or just serve the fruits dressed with the vinaigrette and herbs for a pure citrus experience.

SERVES 4 (AS A SIDE)
6 oranges or blood oranges
4 clementines
1 grapefruit
fresh mint and basil, roughly chopped
baby spinach leaves, to serve (optional)
toasted walnuts, to serve (optional)

VINAIGRETTE:
3 tablespoons olive oil
2 tablespoons red vinegar
1 teaspoon honey or agave syrup
½ teaspoon salt

Whisk together all the ingredients for the vinaigrette in a small bowl until well blended.

To prepare the citrus fruits, take each fruit in turn and slice off the top and bottom, just deep enough to expose the flesh. Sit the fruit firmly on your chopping board and slice downwards, following the curve of the fruit, to cut away the peel, white pith and thin skin on the outside of the fruit, turning the fruit as you continue to work around it. Then slice each fruit crossways into rounds 5mm thick.

Arrange the fruit rounds on a serving plate, drizzle with the vinaigrette and sprinkle with the herbs. Serve with spinach and walnuts if you like.

VE Opt for agave syrup.
GF ✓

Seared Brussels Sprouts with Pomegranate

Strikingly emerald green and ruby in colour, this dish is certain to add festive flair to any table. The earthy brassica taste of Brussels sprouts marries particularly well with the tart sweetness of pomegranate, and frying the sprouts in ghee or butter (or olive oil for a vegan alternative) with garlic gives a boost to their flavour.

SERVES 6 AS A SIDE
2 tablespoons lemon juice
1 teaspoon honey or agave syrup
2 tablespoons pomegranate juice
ghee, butter or olive oil, for frying
2 garlic cloves, crushed
800g Brussel sprouts, trimmed
    and halved
100g pomegranate seeds
salt and freshly ground black pepper,
    to taste

Mix together the lemon juice, honey or agave syrup and pomegranate juice in a small bowl and set aside.

Heat a frying pan over a medium-high heat. Add a generous amount of ghee, butter or olive oil and the garlic and fry the sprouts, cut-side down, for 2 minutes without disturbing. Flip the sprouts over, season with salt and pepper and drizzle with the lemon juice mixture, then fry for a further 5 minutes, ensuring that they cook evenly on their rounded side.

Transfer to a serving dish and sprinkle with the pomegranate seeds.

VE Opt for agave syrup and olive oil.
GF ✓

Endive and Pear Gratin

Endive gratins are hugely popular in the Netherlands, Belgium and northern France. My version is topped with slices of sweet pear and pine nuts. You can adjust the cooking cream and cheese to your preference.

SERVES 6
olive oil, for greasing and drizzling
5 endives, halved
1 small firm pear, cored and sliced
3 garlic cloves, minced
250ml cooking cream of your choice
100ml plant-based or dairy milk
¾ teaspoon salt, plus extra to taste
¼ teaspoon freshly ground black pepper
100g Parmesan, finely grated or
    rawmesan (see page 28)
thyme sprigs
a handful of pine nuts

Preheat the oven to 220°C/gas mark 7. Grease an ovenproof dish and arrange the endive snugly in a single layer. Add the pear slices.

Combine the garlic, cream, milk, salt, pepper and thyme in a saucepan. Bring to a boil and lower the temperature to simmer. Stir and let simmer for 2 minutes. Pour over the endives and pear. Press the endive and pear down into the gratin so everything is covered with cream and bake for 25 minutes.

Sprinkle with cheese, add a few thyme sprigs and pine nuts and bake for a further 10 minutes. Drizzle with olive oil and salt lightly before serving warm.

VE Use vegan cooking cream and cheese and plant-based milk.
GF ✓

Puffed Potatoes

These potatoes are roasted long enough to develop a puffed appearance, which gives them an extra delicious taste. Serve them as a side or with lentil meatballs (see page 56).

SERVES 6
500g waxy potatoes, cut into thick wedges
olive oil
salt
1 tablespoon thyme leaves

Preheat the oven to 220°C/gas mark 7. Put the potato wedges in an ovenproof dish, toss with the olive oil, salt and thyme and roast for 40–45 minutes.

VE ✓
GF ✓

Beetroot Ravioli with Winter Pesto Sauce

SERVES 4–6

BEETROOT FILLING:
2 large beetroot, washed and peeled
100g grated Parmesan or rawmesan
    (see page 28)
50g panko breadcrumbs

FRESH PASTA DOUGH:
200g plain flour
150g semolina flour, plus extra for
    dusting
large pinch of salt
4 medium organic eggs, lightly beaten

WINTER PESTO SAUCE:
2 handfuls of winter green leaves (stalks
    removed), such as kale, cavolo nero
    (black cabbage or kale) or spinach
juice of 1 lemon
2 garlic cloves, crushed
50g Parmesan, grated
75ml extra virgin olive oil
a handful of pistachio nuts or pine nuts
3 tablespoons mascarpone or crème
    fraîche
salt, to taste

TO FINISH:
pinch of salt
olive oil
a few drops of truffle oil (optional)

Tip
*Using wonton wrappers instead of making
the pasta is a handy shortcut if you're
running out of time.*

Embrace the season's hearty flavours by serving up beautiful plates of beetroot ravioli with a pesto sauce made from winter greens. Roasting the beets mellows their earthiness and brings out their sweetness. Serve as a main dish or a side.

Put the beetroots in a food processor with the Parmesan or rawmesan and panko breadcrumbs and whizz to a grainy paste. Remove from the food processor and set aside.

Make the pasta dough. Mix together the flours and salt in a mixing bowl. Make a well in the centre, add the eggs to the well and, using your hands, gradually mix the egg with the flour into a dough. Knead the dough on a work surface for about 3–4 minutes until smooth. Wrap the dough in clingfilm and leave to rest at room temperature for 30 minutes.

Meanwhile, make the pesto sauce. Put the winter greens in a bowl, sprinkle over the lemon juice and massage with your hands for a couple of minutes until the leaves have softened. Add to the food processor with the remaining pesto ingredients and whizz until smooth. Transfer to a saucepan ready to heat up.

To make the ravioli, dust some clean tea towels and a work surface generously with semolina flour. Divide the pasta dough into quarters and keep those you aren't working with covered with clingfilm. Take one quarter and roll out on the prepared work surface into an even thin sheet about 2mm thick. Working quickly, cut the sheet into rounds using a 7cm cutter. Add 1 teaspoon of the filling to the centre of each round, then brush the edges with water, fold one side over the filling to make a semicircular pouch and press the edges together lightly to seal. Once sealed, immediately transfer the ravioli to a floured tea towel. Repeat with the remainder of the dough.

Bring a large saucepan filled with water to the boil. Meanwhile, heat a large frying pan over a low heat and add a drizzle of olive oil. Add the salt and a drizzle of olive oil to the boiling water and cook the ravioli, in batches, for 2 minutes. Remove the cooked ravioli with a slotted spoon and transfer to the frying pan to keep warm until all the pasta is cooked.

While the pasta is cooking, heat the pesto sauce over a low heat and simmer for 2 minutes. Serve the ravioli with the pesto sauce and a few drops of truffle oil, if using.

VE Use vegan wonton wrappers instead of pasta dough, and opt for rawmesan (see page 28) and vegan crème fraîche.
GF Use gluten-free dried breadcrumbs instead of panko, and gluten-free wonton wrappers instead of pasta dough.

You can replace the kuzu with another thickening agent, such as arrowroot, or add vegan cooking cream or double cream for extra creaminess.

Hasselback Celeriac Roast Steak with Mushroom and Shallot Gravy

SERVES 6

1 celeriac, about 800g

HERB AND MUSTARD RUB:

70g panko breadcrumbs

3 tablespoons almond butter

2 tablespoons thyme leaves

1 tablespoon rosemary leaves

1 tablespoon lemon juice

3 garlic cloves, crushed

¾ teaspoon salt

3 tablespoons olive oil

1 tablespoon mustard

1 tablespoon red miso paste (aka miso) or brown rice miso paste (genmai)

MUSHROOM AND SHALLOT GRAVY:

1 tablespoon kuzu (optional)

2 tablespoons cold water (if using kuzu)

30g butter or 2 tablespoons olive oil

70g mixed mushrooms, such as shiitake and oyster, finely chopped

2 shallots, finely chopped

1 tablespoon chopped tarragon

50ml dry sherry or sake, or other sweet wine

250ml vegetable stock

Hasselback potatoes have been popular in Sweden since the 50s when it was first served in Hasselbacken, a restaurant in Sweden. The hasselback technique means cutting scores through potatoes adding an extra texture to the bite, and it can be used on a variety of root vegetables and squashes. Celeriac may have an unflattering rough exterior, but it makes an impressive roast, as the flesh within has a lot of character – more than most other roots, in fact – with an earthy yet clean and sharp celery-like flavour that is mellowed and sweetened with roasting. I serve it with a creamy mushroom and shallot gravy for a balance of texture and bite.

Put all the ingredients for the herb and mustard rub in a blender or food processor and whizz until well combined. Set aside.

Preheat the oven to 190°C/gas mark 5. Trim the sprouty roots from the celeriac and scrub it clean. Sit on a sheet of foil. Using a sharp knife, cut the celeriac into thin slices down from the top to about three-quarters of the way through the celeriac, leaving the last quarter at the base uncut. Brush the celeriac generously with the rub, working it down inside the cuts as deep as you can go. Wrap in the foil and roast for 2–2½ hours until the celeriac is cooked through, opening up the foil wrapping for the last 30 minutes of roasting.

Meanwhile, make the mushroom and shallot gravy. If you want to thicken the gravy, crush the kuzu pieces using a pestle and mortar, then dissolve it in the cold water and set aside. Heat a frying pan over a medium-high heat. Add the butter or olive oil and fry the mushrooms and shallots with the tarragon for 7–8 minutes, stirring frequently. Stir in the sherry, sake or wine and the stock, reduce the heat to low and leave to simmer for 4–5 minutes. Add the kuzu mixture, if using, and whisk until combined and smooth. Simmer for a couple of minutes until thickened. Set aside and reheat before serving.

To serve, drizzle a few tablespoons of the reheated mushroom and shallot gravy on a serving platter and add the roasted celeriac. Serve the celeriac in slices, drizzled with the gravy.

VE Opt for olive oil.

GF Use gluten-free dried breadcrumbs instead of panko.

Date and Beetroot Chocolate Cake with Lingonberry Glaze

MAKES 1 CAKE; SERVES 8

2–3 beetroot (about 200g), peeled and chopped

8 dried Medjool dates, soaked in water for 30 minutes–2 hours, then drained and pitted

180ml plant-based or dairy milk

2 tablespoons lemon juice

2 teaspoons vanilla extract

225g spelt flour or flour of choice

40g raw cacao powder or cocoa powder

1 teaspoon bicarbonate of soda

1 teaspoon baking powder

¾ teaspoon salt, or more to taste

80g coconut oil or butter, melted, plus extra for greasing

150g coconut sugar

3 medium organic eggs or 3 bananas, mashed

CHOCOLATE CASHEW BUTTER CREAM:

200g raw cashew nuts, presoaked in warm water for an hour, then drained

100ml cashew or other plant-based milk

50ml agave syrup

2 tablespoons raw cacao or cocoa powder

1 teaspoon vanilla extract

pinch of salt

LINGONBERRY GLAZE

100ml coconut milk

2 tablespoons lingonberry powder (or other flavouring powder or smooth berry purée)

70ml agave syrup

2 teaspoons vanilla extract

100ml coconut oil

I prefer moderately sweetened desserts to sugar bombs. I like to 'cut' the sweetness with grown-up flavours such as nuts, coffee and, as in this recipe, earthy beetroot, which gives a deep, juicy tone to this take on a red velvet cake. The cacao or cocoa and beetroot are balanced by the modest sweetness of the dates and coconut sugar, and a luscious lingonberry glaze to continue the velvet theme. This is a beautiful cake to serve at any time of year.

Preheat the oven to 180°C/gas mark 4. Grease a 20cm round cake tin with coconut oil or butter and line the base with baking paper.

Put the beetroot, dates, milk, lemon juice and vanilla extract in a food processor and whizz until smooth. Sift together the flour, cacao or cocoa, bicarbonate of soda, baking powder and salt into a bowl and set aside.

Using a hand-held electric mixer or a balloon whisk, beat together the coconut oil or butter and coconut sugar in a mixing bowl until smooth. Add the eggs one by one or the bananas (or other egg replacer) a third at a time, beating well after each addition. Combine the beetroot mixture, flour mixture and coconut oil or butter mixture by adding a small quantity of each mixture at a time to a separate large mixing bowl while beating constantly. Pour the cake mixture into the greased tin and bake for 60 minutes or until a skewer inserted into the centre of the cake comes out clean. Remove from the oven and allow to cool in the tin.

To make the chocolate cashew butter cream, whizz the ingredients together until smooth in a food processor. Cover and refrigerate until ready to use. It will keep in the fridge for two days.

Meanwhile, prepare the lingonberry glaze. Mix the glaze ingredients, except the coconut oil, in a blender until smooth. Add the coconut oil, a tablespoon at a time, blending until smooth.

To assemble, remove the cake from its tin and peel away the lining paper, then place on a serving platter. Halve the cake carefully. Using a flat spatula, spread the cashew butter cream evenly over the base cake. Place the other half on top and drizzle with lingonberry icing.

VE Opt for plant-based milk, coconut oil and vegan egg replacer.

GF The cake is not gluten free.

Lingonberry powder

Lingonberry powder is made with ligonberries and has emerged recently as an exciting powder to use in desserts and other dishes where sour, tangy flavour is needed. Lingonberries are a popular ingredient in Scandinavian cooking and the dried powder is a popular choice in place of Brazilian açaí powder when making smoothies.

4. CELEBRATION SALADS

Salads were once the mere sideshow of the dining experience, but not any more.
As these recipes demonstrate, salads have now moved centre stage to become star dishes in
their own right, exploding with flavour, colour and texture. Dressings are key to creating a great
salad, with their ability to bring out the full flavour of ingredients and also to bring them together.
But they perform a fine balancing act between mellow and tangy, salty and sweet, so
always adjust the components to your taste before serving.
Salads invite you to be flexible, so adopt the traditional Japanese wabi-sabi approach of
going with the natural flow and making the best of what you've got. So if you're missing
an ingredient or two, simply substitute ones that have similar qualities, for
example sweetness, crispiness or fresh fragrance.

Sweet Potatoes, Kale and Spicy Chickpeas with Lemon Almond Dressing

SERVES 4

SWEET POTATOES AND SPICY
   CHICKPEAS:
1 medium sweet potato, peeled and cut
   into small wedges
2 tablespoons olive oil
salt, to taste
½ teaspoon ground cumin
400g can chickpeas, drained and patted
   dry with kitchen paper
½ teaspoon sweet paprika
¼ teaspoon dried chilli flakes

KALE:
olive oil, for frying
75g kale or cavolo nero (black cabbage or
   kale), stalks removed and chopped
salt and freshly ground black pepper,
   to taste

LEMON ALMOND DRESSING:
150ml plant-based milk
3 tablespoons almond butter
2 tablespoons shoyu soy or tamari sauce
1 teaspoon lemon juice
2 garlic cloves
1 teaspoon honey or agave syrup
½ teaspoon crushed garlic (or grated
   fresh ginger for a variation)

TO SERVE:
3 tablespoons pomegranate seeds
75g baby spinach leaves
2 carrots, julienned
½ red onion, sliced
2 slices of radish, to decorate (optional)

This filling salad offers a variety of flavours and textures. Wilted kale and meltingly soft sweet potato make a great combination with the spicy roasted chickpeas. Finished with pomegranate seeds, avocado and red onion, this sumptuous salad covers all the bases.

Preheat the oven to 230°C/gas mark 8 and line one or two baking trays with baking paper. Toss the sweet potato wedges with 1 tablespoon of the olive oil, a sprinkle of salt and the cumin in a bowl until well mixed. In a separate bowl, toss the chickpeas with the remaining 1 tablespoon olive oil, the paprika and chilli flakes. Arrange the sweet potato wedges and chickpeas separately in a single layer on the lined baking tray (use two trays if necessary) and roast for 30 minutes.

Heat a frying pan over a medium-high heat. Add a drizzle of olive oil and fry the kale or cavolo nero until wilted. Sprinkle with a little salt and pepper.

Whizz together all the ingredients for the Lemon Almond Dressing with a hand blender in a jug until well blended.

In a large serving bowl, combine everything and serve with the Lemon Almond Dressing.

VE Opt for agave syrup.
GF Opt for tamari sauce.

Mint Avocado Smoothie

Give green smoothies a mint edge!

———

SERVES 1
1 avocado, chopped
2 tablespoons almond butter
2 Medjool dates, pitted
2 teaspoons chlorella or wheatgrass
3 tablespoons chopped fresh mint
20g fresh spinach
200ml plant-based milk
pinch of salt

Blend all the ingredients in a food processor until smooth, adding a little more plant-based milk if you want a thinner consistency.

VE ✓ GF ✓

Beet Carrot Smoothie

———

Beetroot blends deliciously with raspberries and carrot. I use raspberries to freshen up the flavour of the beetroot, but you can use other berries.

———

SERVES 1
½ medium carrot
1 small red beetroot, peeled and finely grated
150ml plant-based milk
50g raspberries
50g presoaked cashew nuts
1 Medjool date, pitted
pinch of salt

Blend all the ingredients in a food processor until smooth, adding a little more plant-based milk if you want a thinner consistency.

VE ✓ GF ✓

Cauliflower Smoothie

———

Cauli and turmeric, dates and ginger make this golden smoothie stand out.

———

SERVES 1
50g cauliflower florets
1 ripe small banana
2 Medjool dates, pitted
1 teaspoon ground or fresh turmeric
pinch of freshly ground black pepper
¼ teaspoon ground cinnamon
½ teaspoon ground or fresh ginger
200ml coconut or other plant-based milk

Blend all the ingredients in a food processor until smooth, adding a little more plant-based milk if you want a thinner consistency.

VE ✓ GF ✓

New Moon Salad

———

In mindfulness and yoga, the new moon represents a time to start anew and many people eat nourishing and cleansing foods during this time. This salad is filled with protein-rich quinoa and healthy fats from walnuts and avocado. If you want the full health bar experience, serve with nourishing smoothies or fresh juices.

———

SERVES 4
200g quinoa, rinsed
200g your favourite beans (I used cooked edamame and black beans)
2 avocados, sliced
50g radishes, any variety, thinly sliced
2 handfuls of mixed sprouts and microshoots (I use bean sprouts, beet and radish sprouts and green microshoots)
75g baby spinach leaves
2 medium carrots, julienned
2 handfuls of walnuts

NEW MOON DRESSING:
1 teaspoon chlorella or wheatgrass
3 tablespoon fresh coriander, chopped
1 garlic clove, crushed
½ teaspoon salt
1 tablespoon nutritional yeast
1 teaspoon lemon or lime juice
1 tablespoon olive oil or other cold-pressed oil
1 teaspoon honey or agave syrup
100g crème fraîche or vegan crème fraîche or Greek yogurt

Add the quinoa to a pan and add double the amount of water to the quinoa. Cook for 15 minutes, drain and cool. Mix the ingredients for the dressing together. Divide the quinoa and the rest of the salad ingredients between bowls or arrange in one large serving bowl. Serve with a drizzle of the dressing.

VE Use vegan crème fraîche GF ✓

Farmer's Market and Noodle Salad

SERVES 4

vegetable oil, for frying

300g firm organic tofu, drained and pressed, cut into bite-size pieces

2 tablespoons shoyu soy or tamari sauce

2 tablespoons agave syrup

¼ teaspoon chilli powder

400g mixed vegetables, such as carrots, cabbage (I use pak choi), kale or cavolo nero (black cabbage or kale), broccoli, cauliflower or green beans, peeled and stalks removed where necessary and separated into florets or cut into bite-sized pieces

250g dried noodles of your choice

2 handfuls of fresh beansprouts or other sprouts

a handful of fresh coriander, chopped

2 tablespoons sesame seeds

salt and freshly ground black pepper, to taste

SOY AND CHILLI DRESSING:

100ml shoyu soy or tamari sauce

2 tabelspoons toasted sesame oil

1 garlic clove, crushed

2 tablespoons almond or cashew butter

2 tablespoons gochujang, chilli paste, sriracha, or other chilli sauce

juice of 1 lime

2 teaspoons coconut sugar

When you're planning to cook for a gathering, it can be tricky if you have a strict ingredient list to shop for because if you can't get hold of key ingredients, despite their being in season, you're faced with replanning a whole meal at the last minute. The solution is to rely on store-cupboard staples as a basis, such as noodles, and reliable flavourings for making sauces that you can easily customise to work with whatever fresh vegetables are available on the day. I love farmer's markets where I can source both exceptional fresh organic ingredients, such as beautiful broccoli, cabbage and carrots, along with other top-quality ingredients to keep in store. This Asian-inspired market salad, a sprouted version of Pad Thai, uses a feisty soy sauce dressing to bring added flavour to mixed fresh vegetables of your choice. Top with crunchy beansprouts for extra texture interest.

Heat a frying pan over a medium-high heat. Add a drizzle of vegetable oil and fry the tofu until golden brown on all sides, about 2–3 minutes. Mix soy and agave and chilli pepper and splash on the tofu, fry for another minute and remove from heat. Season to taste with salt and pepper and leave to cool.

Prepare the vegetables that need to be cooked. If using broccoli or cauliflower florets, steam them for 4 minutes. If using sturdy cabbage, such as kale or cavolo nero, fry in a little drizzle of oil over a medium-high heat for 1–2 minutes until wilted. Green beans can be steamed as for the broccoli or cauliflower or blanched in boiling water for 1 minute. Allow to cool.

Cook the noodles according to the packet instructions, then drain and rinse in cold water. Meanwhile, whizz together all the ingredients for the soy and chilli dressing with a handheld blender in a jug until well blended. Divide the noodles on serving plates or bowls with the prepared veggies and tofu. Add the sprouts and microshoots, and drizzle with the soy and chilli dressing. Sprinkle with sesame seeds and serve.

VE Use egg-free noodles.
GF Opt for tamari sauce and sriracha or another gluten-free chilli sauce; use gluten-free noodles such as soba buckwheat noodles.

Wabi-sabi Salad

SERVES 4

200g brown rice or Japanese or sushi rice

vegetable oil or ghee, for frying

200g oyster or shiitake mushrooms, sliced

½ teaspoon shichimi togarashi or dried chilli flakes

250g freshly shelled edamame beans

2 tablespoons furikake (see page 166 for homemade)

200g firm smoked tofu, cut into matchsticks

1–2 watermelon radishes or Chioggia beetroot, trimmed, peeled and cut into thin sticks

2 carrots, peeled and cut into matchsticks

½ dragon fruit, flesh scooped out and diced

1 avocado, diced

WABI-SABI SAUCE:

50ml shoyu soy or tamari sauce

50ml rice vinegar

1 teaspoon honey or agave syrup

1 teaspoon freshly grated ginger

1 tablespoon almond or cashew butter

1 tablespoon sesame oil

1 teaspoon nutritional yeast or 1 garlic clove, crushed (optional)

TO GARNISH:

black sesame seeds

ready-toasted nori, cut into thin strips

This salad is a fun and delicious way to enjoy the essence of sushi for those who love it but don't love the bother of rolling nori sheets. Wabi-sabi is a traditional Japanese philosophy that celebrates the beauty of imperfection, so in that spirit, feel free to change and customise your salad using different vegetables and grains. I've added mushrooms, which fall outside of the usual sushi flavour palette but deliver a umami boost to the dish.

The sauce and furikake (if you make your own) can be prepared a day or a few hours ahead of serving. The rice can be cooked a day ahead, and stored sealed once it's cooled, in the fridge. Cut the vegetables just before assembly.

———

Prepare and cook the rice according to the packet instructions (or according to the instructions on page 16 if using Japanese or sushi rice), then drain if necessary and leave to cool.

Meanwhile, heat a frying pan to a medium-high heat. Add a drizzle of vegetable oil and fry the oyster mushrooms, leave undisturbed for 2 minutes, then, fry stirring for 5 minutes or until they have shrunk in size and the excess moisture has evaporated. Sprinkle with the shichimi togarashi or chilli flakes.

Cook the edamame beans in a saucepan of boiling water for 3–5 minutes until tender. Drain and fresh under cold running water.

Whizz together all the ingredients for the wabi-sabi sauce with a hand blender in a jug until well blended.

Transfer the cooled cooked rice to a large serving bowl, then mix the furikake through the rice. Arrange all the prepared ingredients in a bowl and garnish with black sesame seeds and nori strips before serving with the wabi-sabi sauce.

Tip

Add ¼ teaspoon of wasabi paste to the sauce for a hot variation.

VE Make your own furikake (see page 166) or look for tuna-free furikake if buying ready-made; opt for agave syrup.

GF Opt for tamari sauce.

Watermelon and Chioggia Beetroot with Miso Wow Sauce

SERVES 4

1–2 Chioggia beetroot, peeled thinly sliced and cut to bite-sized triangle pieces

200g watermelon flesh, cut into bite-sized triangle pieces

MISO WOW SAUCE

1½ tablespoons red miso paste (aka miso) or brown rice miso paste (genmai)

1½ teaspoons drained capers

1 tablespoon shoyu soy or tamari sauce

1 teaspoon lemon juice

⅓ teaspoon honey or agave syrup

2 tablespoons nutritional yeast or grated Parmesan

100ml water

1 teaspoon kuzu (optional)

¼ teaspoon freshly ground black pepper

100g mayonnaise or crème fraîche

1 tablespoon microgreens, such as red vein sorrel leaves and shiso leaves or use delicate herbs, such as baby basil leaves, to serve

1 teaspoon black sesame seeds

This vibrant sharing salad combines sweet watermelon with earthy Chioggia beetroot and offers fresh sweet and savoury flavours to tease the appetite. But it's actually the sauce that's the real star in this ensemble. You can use this creamy miso sauce warm or cold with any variety of cooked or raw vegetables. I call it Miso wow sauce!

To make the sauce, put all the ingredients, except the mayonnaise, in a food processor and whizz until smooth. Transfer to a small saucepan and bring to the boil, stirring, then turn off the heat. Allow to cool slightly and whisk in the mayonnaise or crème fraîche. The sauce can be made a day in advance and kept, tightly covered or in an airtight container, in the fridge. Before serving, heat up the sauce, whisking it until smooth and adding a little water to loosen the consistency if necessary. Leave to cool slightly before serving.

Arrange the Chioggia beetroot and watermelon slices on a serving dish, drizzle with the sauce and top with microgreens and black sesame seeds.

VE Opt for vegan mayonnaise or vegan crème fraîche; use agave syrup and nutritional yeast.

GF Opt for tamari sauce.

Tip

I've used kuzu here as a thickener, which gives a lovely smoothness and shine to sauces and gels without any weird aftertaste, but you can use arrowroot or another thickener if you prefer. Alternatively, add vegan or dairy crème fraîche to the sauce instead.

Pea Shoots and Courgette Salad with Hot Tamari Tempeh

SERVES 4

250g best-quality tempeh, cut into
    bite-sized pieces
vegetable oil, for frying

DRESSING:

75ml shoyu soy or tamari sauce
25ml mirin
25ml rice vinegar
1½ teaspoons freshly grated ginger
1 tablespoon coconut sugar or agave syrup
¼ teaspoon salt

TEMPEH SEASONING:

2 tablespoons shoyu soy or tamari sauce
1 tablespoon coconut sugar or agave syrup
1 teaspoon sriracha or other hot sauce

4 spring onions, chopped
½ cucumber, chopped
1 large avocado, sliced
2 medium courgettes, spiralised
a handful of peashoots

This very fresh and cool salad combines spiralised courgette with cucumber, avocado, spring onions and tender raw pea shoots. It's a perfect spring and summer salad, but also an option to complement heartier dishes when you need to balance them with something less heavy. The tempeh adds a spicy flavour and extra interest to the salad. A light and sweetened tamari and ginger dressing gives an extra edge to the taste. You can use other delicate shoots or sprouts instead of pea shoots and use tofu or chickpeas instead of tempeh.

Mix the ingredients for the dressing together, and set aside. Mix the ingredients for the tempeh seasoning together and set aside.

Heat a frying pan over a medium-high heat. Add a drizzle of vegetable oil and fry the tempeh. Let the pieces fry until the surface is seared and golden before stirring and turning the pieces around, about 4–5 minutes. When the tempeh is nicely golden on all sides, splash the seasoning mixture over the pieces and allow the liquids to be absorbed before removing the tempeh from the heat.

Divide the salad between serving bowls or mix the ingredients in one large bowl. Serve with the tempeh and dressing.

VE ✓
GF Opt for tamari sauce.

Nordic
Nacho Salad

SERVES 4

COTTAGE CHEESE AND
    HORSERADISH DIP
1 tablespoon horseradish sauce, and
    more to taste (this can be substituted
    with 1 teaspoon chilli paste or
    wasabi paste)
¼ teaspoon salt, and more to taste
1 tablespoon olive oil
100g cottage cheese
1 tablespoon lemon juice

4 tortillas or flatbreads of choice (you can
    also use thin Swedish crispbreads –
    they don't need toasting)
75g baby spinach or other green leaves
250g chanterelles or other mushrooms
olive oil or butter, for frying
3 tablespoons finely chopped chives
salt and fresh ground black pepper

VE Use vegan soft cheese or vegan crème fraîche
instead of cottage cheese.
GF Opt for corn not wheat tortillas or use gluten-
free flatbreads or crackers.

Chanterelles are highly rated in Scandinavia and mostly prepared
in a simple manner to let the pure flavour sing. In this salad, fried
chanterelles are layered with spinach, chives and a zesty horseradish
cream. For a crispy contrast, toasted tortillas or flatbreads add a crunch
to the dish; if you want to go the whole way with the Scandinavian theme,
you can use thin knäckebröd, like the sesame and sea salt cracker from
the brand Wasa.

Mix the ingredients for the dip until smooth. Cut the tortilla bread into smaller
pieces. Heat a frying pan and toast the tortilla pieces until crispy on both sides,
about 20–30 seconds on each side. Remove and add to the serving plate.

Heat the frying pan over a medium-high heat and add the chanterelles
without any fat. Fry the chanterelles, stirring every few seconds, until they
release their liquids. When the liquids have reduced in the pan, add a drizzle
of olive oil or a tablespoon of butter and fry quickly to coat, sprinkle with salt
and pepper and transfer to the bowl with spinach. Dot with the cottage cheese
and horseradish dip so that it is evenly distributed. Sprinkle with chives,
season with salt and pepper and serve.

Pumpkin, Wild Rice and Lemongrass Salad

SERVES 4

200g wild rice
1 medium pumpkin or Delicata squash,
   halved, seeds and membrane
   removed, peeled and cut into wedges
groundnut or vegetable oil, for drizzling
50g roasted hazelnuts
2 avocados, sliced
a handful of coriander and flat-leaf
   parsley leaves
salt and freshly ground black pepper,
   to taste

LEMONGRASS DRESSING:
100ml rice vinegar
2 tablespoons shoyu soy or tamari sauce
1 tablespoon toasted sesame oil
1 teaspoon fresh lime juice
2 tablespoons coconut sugar
1 lemongrass stalk, white part only,
   tough outer layers removed and
   finely chopped
1 garlic clove, crushed
1 teaspoon freshly grated ginger
1 teaspoon finely chopped red chilli
salt, to taste

TO SERVE
lime wedges
shiso leaves or other micro greens
   (optional)

VE ✓
GF Opt for tamari sauce.

Here is a salad full of dramatic contrasts. Sweet roasted pumpkin or squash wedges are enhanced by a tangy Asian-style lemongrass dressing, with wild rice providing a striking black colour and chewy texture. Wild rice has to be dried and roasted before it's edible and this process gives the grains their extra-deep nutty flavour and hue. It's often sold mixed with regular long-grain rice, sometimes with the addition of gluten-containing flavourings, so check the details on the packet for gluten content and different cooking times. Roasted hazelnuts add a harmonising element to finish.

Cook the wild rice according to the packet instructions (usually simmered for about 45 minutes), then drain.

Preheat the oven to 200°C/gas mark 6. Line a baking tray with baking paper. Put the pumpkin or squash wedges in a bowl, drizzle with oil and sprinkle with salt and pepper, then toss to coat. Arrange in a single layer on the lined baking tray and roast for 25 minutes. Flip the wedges over and roast on the other side for 10 minutes or until golden and tender.

Meanwhile, whisk together all the ingredients for the lemongrass dressing in a bowl until well combined.

To serve, toss the roasted pumpkin or squash with the cooked wild rice, top with the roasted hazelnuts, avocado and herbs and drizzle with the lemongrass dressing. Serve warm with lime wedges for squeezing and shiso leaves, if you wish.

Jackfruit Bulgogi Salad

SERVES 4

2 tablespoons toasted sesame oil

2 tablespoons rice vinegar or citrus juice

salt and freshly ground black pepper,
    to taste

400g Jackfruit Bulgogi (see page 125)

2 avocados, diced

1 Asian pear or regular firm pear, cored
    and cut into strips

4 spring onions, sliced

60g baby spinach or other green
    salad leaves

50g toasted cashew nuts

1 tablespoon sesame seeds

This salad is packed with flavour! Using fried jackfruit, marinated with shoyu and chilli, as a delicious savoury element in a fresh green salad. Pear, avocado and spinach add a cool contrast and cashew nuts the extra crunch. You will find the method for preparing the Jackfruit Bulgogi on page 125. The Bulgogi is best served warm but you can eat this salad warm or cold. It's an excellent dish to take to a barbecue or potluck supper.

Mix the toasted sesame oil and rice vinegar together and set aside. Arrange the rest of the ingredients in a bowl and serve with the dressing.

VE ✓

GF Opt for tamari for the Jackfruit Bulgogi.

Herbed Beetroot, Lentil and Feta Salad

SERVES 4

4 medium beetroots, washed
8 small carrots, scrubbed and cut
    into lengths
olive oil, for roasting
1 tablespoon thyme leaves
1 litre vegetable stock or water
2 handfuls of baby spinach leaves
200g feta or soft fresh goat's cheese
a handful of tarragon leaves,
    finely chopped
extra virgin olive oil, for drizzling
200g Puy lentils, rinsed and drained
salt and freshly ground black pepper,
    to taste

DIJON DRESSING:

50ml olive oil
2 tablespoons red vine vinegar
1 tablespoon mayonnaise
1 teaspoon Dijon mustard
1 teaspoon honey or agave syrup
2 garlic cloves, crushed
1 teaspoon thyme leaves
½ teaspoon salt
freshly ground black pepper, to taste

I like to combine earthy-tasting lentils and beetroot with bold flavours, here with a mustard-spiked dressing and tangy cheese. There's a French thread running through the ingredients in this salad, from the Dijon mustard to the Puy lentils and the tarragon and aromatic fresh thyme, but it's a dish that blends easily with other dishes for sharing or as a side dish, as well as being sufficiently substantial to be served as a main.

Preheat the oven to 200°C/gas mark 6. Wrap the beetroots individually in foil and sit on a baking tray. Put the carrots in a bowl, drizzle with olive oil and sprinkle with salt, then toss to coat. Transfer to the baking tray and sprinkle with the thyme. Roast for about 45 minutes or until the beetroot are tender, but keep an eye on the carrots and remove them from the oven earlier if they look done. Leave the beetroot and carrots to cool, then peel the beetroot and cut into small wedges.

Meanwhile, bring the stock or water to the boil in a saucepan. Add the lentils, reduce the heat and simmer gently for 20–25 minutes until tender. Drain and rinse in cold water. Shake off the excess moisture and leave to air-dry for a few minutes.

Whisk together all the ingredients for the Dijon dressing in a bowl until well combined.

Tip the lentils into a large serving bowl, drizzle with the dressing and season to taste with salt and pepper. Add the baby spinach and the roasted beetroot and carrots, then crumble the cheese over the top. Sprinkle with the tarragon and add a drizzle of extra virgin olive oil.

VE Opt for vegan feta-style or soft cheese,
vegan mayonnaise and agave syrup.
GF Opt for gluten-free mayonnaise.

Strawberry Summer Salad

SERVES 4

250g cherry tomatoes, chopped

1 small red onion, diced small

75g salad leaves

100g strawberries, halved

50g roasted nuts, such as walnuts,
   pecans or almonds

1 avocado, cut into small pieces

50g croutons

DRESSING:

50ml balsamic vinegar

2 garlic cloves, crushed in ¾ teaspoon
   salt

1½ teaspoons honey or agave syrup or
   other sweetener

50ml extra virgin olive oil

1 teaspoon dijon mustard

I make this salad as soon as there are fresh strawberries in season. It's the perfect side dish that goes well with literally anything savoury. Adding strawberries to a regular green salad with tomatoes makes it instantly festive. The sweet berries add a lovely contrast to garlic and onions, while croutons and nuts give a pleasing crunch. In the winter, swap the strawberries for dried fruit, such as apriciots, figs or raisins.

Mix the dressing ingredients together in a large bowl. Add the tomatoes and red onion and toss to coat. Leave for 20 minutes or longer. Toss with the rest of the ingredients and serve.

VE Opt for agave syrup.

GF Opt for gluten-free croutons, or omit.

5. HEARTY MEALS

Stews, curries and bakes are perfect choices for gatherings - fuss free and brimming with melding flavours as a result of all the ingredients being cooked up together in the pot or dish. The cooking methods involved also contribute to a satisfying taste experience, with vegetables releasing an abundance of flavour when roasted in the oven or slow-cooked on the hob.

With these recipes, you can treat your guests to vegetable-enriched takes on hearty classics from around the globe, including a sweet and fragrant Tunisian stew of aubergines and tomatoes and a rainbow-coloured feast of curry dishes. This is comfort food at its best!

Golden Kerala Curry

SERVES 4–6

1kg mixed vegetables, such as peppers,
    baby aubergines, green beans and
    courgettes, chopped or sliced
ghee or vegetable oil, for frying
4 shallots, finely chopped
500ml vegetable stock
800ml coconut milk
3 tablespoons light soy or tamari sauce
1½ tablespoons coconut or brown sugar
a handful of fresh coriander, chopped

SPICE PASTE:

1 tablespoon ghee or coconut oil
5 garlic cloves, crushed
2 teaspoons fresh lemongrass or
    lemongrass paste
½ red chilli, deseeded, or more to taste
1 tablespoon grated fresh ginger
¾ tablespoon ground turmeric
2 teaspoons garam masala
1 teaspoon ground coriander
¼ teaspoon freshly ground black pepper
¾ tablespoon salt, plus extra to taste

TO SERVE:

fresh coriander
400g cooked rice or other grain
1–2 limes, cut into wedges
yogurt or raita or naan
Indian Carrot Salad (see page 101)

Inspired by the flavours of Kerala, the region of South India known for its many Ayurvedic and yoga schools and for being one of the happiest places on earth according to some studies, this is a stew for nourishing mind, body and spirit! Light and satisfying at the same time, it is flavoured with coconut, turmeric and lemongrass. Don't be deterred by the long list of ingredients, as most are spices or storecupboard staples you probably already have at home. You can choose to make the curry less or more spicy. Add ½ red chilli to start, and more for extra hotness.

The Indian Carrot Salad (see page 101) makes the perfect side dish for this stew, but raita and naan bread work well, too.

Put all the ingredients for the spice paste in a food processor and whizz to a coarse paste. Rub the paste all over the prepared mixed vegetables.

Heat a large heavy-based saucepan or casserole over a medium heat. Add a little ghee or a drizzle of vegetable oil and fry the shallots, stirring, for 4–5 minutes until translucent. Add the vegetables with all the spice paste and a little more ghee or oil, then fry, stirring, for 2–3 minutes. Stir in the stock, coconut milk, soy and sugar and bring to the boil, then reduce the heat and simmer for 15 minutes. Taste and adjust the seasoning with salt, if needed.

Sprinkle coriander over the curry and serve with cooked rice or other grain, along with lime wedges and either yogurt or raita and naan.

VE Opt for coconut oil for the spice paste and
vegetable oil for frying; use vegan yogurt.
GF Opt for tamari sauce; serve with gluten-free
flatbread instead of naan.

Rainbow Curry Table

PILAF:

250g basmati rice, rinsed in several
  changes of cold water until the water
  is clear, then soaked in fresh cold
  water for 30 minutes
500ml water
1 chai tea bag
ghee or vegetable oil, for frying
2 shallots, finely sliced
1 teaspoon ground turmeric
½ teaspoon ground cinnamon
¼ teaspoon freshly ground black pepper
50g toasted almonds, coarsely ground
2 garlic cloves, crushed
a handful of raisins

CHICKPEA AND SPINACH CURRY:

ghee or vegetable oil, for frying
2 shallots, finely diced
2 teaspoon black mustard seeds, toasted
  and ground
1 tablespoon ground coriander
¾ tablespoon garam masala
¾ teaspoon salt, plus extra to taste
300g spinach leaves, roughly chopped
2 x 400g cans chickpeas, rinsed
  and drained
600ml vegetable stock
10g fresh coriander, finely chopped
1 tablespoon lemon juice
1 teaspoon honey or agave syrup

SIMPLE RAITA:

200g yogurt
pinch of salt
pinch of cumin
2 tablespoons grated cucumber (optional)

TO SERVE:

Tandoori Cauliflower (see page 101)
Cherry Chutney (see page 131)
pickles
naan bread

Comforting and full of vibrant flavour, curries win my heart and my stomach every time! The concept of this meal is to serve a table of curries, where the flavours of the different dishes fold into one another beautifully when combined in each guest's bowl. Alternatively, you can cherry pick any one of the components to make and enjoy on its own.

The bold smoky quality of the tandoori cauliflower harmonises well with the fragrant lemony edge of the fresh coriander in the chickpea and spinach curry, while the pilaf is made warmly aromatic and earthy with the spicing of chai tea and therapeutic turmeric.

Take your guests further on the spice trail by adding cherry chutney (see page 131), a fantastic sweet contrast to the savoury curry, and cooling elements to complete the taste experience, such as a tangy yogurt raita, pickles and naan bread.

———

To make the pilaf, drain the rice and put in a saucepan that has a tight-fitting lid, cover with the water and add the tea bag. Bring to the boil, then reduce the heat, cover the pan with the lid and leave to simmer for 10-12 minutes. Turn off the heat, remove the tea bag and leave the rice to stand, uncovered, while you fry the shallots.

Heat a large, wide frying pan over a medium heat. Add a little ghee or vegetable oil and fry the shallots, stirring frequently, for 5-7 minutes until transparent. Add the remaining pilaf ingredients including the cooked rice and fry, stirring, for 3-4 minutes.

To make the chickpea and spinach curry, heat a saucepan that has a lid over a medium-high heat. Add a little ghee or vegetable oil and fry the shallots with the spices and salt, stirring, for 4-5 minutes. Add the spinach and cook, stirring it with the shallot and spices, until wilted. Stir in the remaining curry ingredients, cover the pan with the lid and leave to simmer for 10 minutes. Taste and adjust the seasoning with salt.

To make the raita, simply mix the raita ingredients together in a small bowl.

To assemble the curry table, put the warm pilaf and chickpea and spinach curry in serving dishes, along with accompanying dishes of the Tandoori Cauliflower and Cherry Chutney, plus raita, pickles and naan bread.

VE Opt for vegetable oil for frying and agave syrup for the curry; vegan yogurt for making the Tandoori Cauliflower and raita.
VE Serve with gluten-free flatbread instead of naan.

Tandoori Cauliflower

This dish of mouthwatering cauliflower is coated with a tandoori yogurt marinade spiked with sweet and smoked paprika before baking for an extra depth of flavour. Serve as a side with other curries. Alternatively, turn it into a main meal for four by serving with rice or pilaf (see page 99) and other Indian side dishes such as pickles, raita and naan bread.

SERVES 8
1 cauliflower, divided into florets

TANDOORI YOGURT MARINADE:
300ml Greek yogurt
100ml olive oil
2 tablespoons sweet paprika
1 teaspoon smoked paprika
1 tablespoon plus 1 teaspoon garam masala
2 teaspoons ground turmeric
1 teaspoon salt, plus extra to taste
2 teaspoons agave syrup
¼ teaspoon cayenne pepper, or more to taste

Preheat the oven to 200°C/gas mark 6. Whisk together all the ingredients for the tandoori yogurt marinade in a bowl until smooth. Rub the cauliflower florets with half the marinade and arrange them in a single layer in a large ovenproof dish. Bake for 45–50 minutes.

Towards the end of the baking time, gently heat the remainder of the marinade in a saucepan. When the cauliflower is done, pour the warmed-up marinade over the florets and season to taste with salt and cayenne pepper. The tandoori marinade can be prepared a day ahead and kept, tightly covered, in the fridge.

VE Opt for vegan yogurt.
GF ✓

Indian Carrot Salad

This dish always attracts praise around the table. It's delicious with curries, but will bring a cooling, sweet contrast to many other types of savoury dish. I use baby orange carrots, or rainbow carrots if I can find them.

SERVES 4–6
500g good-quality carrots, peeled
1–2 avocados, cut into wedges
1 small red onion, thinly sliced
a handful of fresh coriander
a handful of mint
a handful of sesame seeds
salt and freshly ground black pepper, to taste

DRESSING:
2½ tablespoons rice vinegar or white wine vinegar
1 tablespoon extra virgin olive oil
1 tablespoon toasted sesame oil
1 garlic clove, crushed
1 teaspoon grated fresh ginger
1 teaspoon ground cumin
½ teaspoon ground coriander

Slice the carrots lengthways into thin ribbons. Arrange the ribbons in a serving dish with the avocado, onion and herbs, then sprinkle with salt and pepper to taste.

Whisk together all the dressing ingredients in a small bowl until smooth, then pour over the salad. Sprinkle with the sesame seeds.

VE ✓ GF ✓

Ribollita

SERVES 4
olive oil, for frying
5 shallots, finely chopped
3 garlic cloves, minced
2 carrots, peeled and finely diced
1 celery stick, finely chopped
pinch of ground fennel seeds
1 tablespoon dried rosemary or thyme
    or a pinch of chilli flakes
¾ teaspoon salt
200g cavolo nero (black cabbage or
    kale), stems removed and leaves
    finely chopped
10g flat-leaf parsley, finely chopped
1 litre good-quality vegetable stock
3 tablespoons red wine
1 teaspoon honey or agave syrup
2 tablespoons grated Parmesan or
    rawmesan (see page 28)
400g can good-quality plum tomatoes
400g can cannellini beans, rinsed
    and drained
extra virgin olive oil, for drizzling
salt and freshly ground black pepper,
    to taste

TO SERVE
200g dry bread, torn into chunks
    (optional)

Ribollita is a well-rounded flavour affair, and one of my all-time favourite dishes. The star ingredient here is cavolo nero, a black cabbage or kale with a deep baritone taste that makes a perfect contrast to tomatoes, bread and beans in this rustic Tuscan farmers' soup. Though filling, it's guaranteed to make your friends and family ask for a second serving. Scoop up!

Heat a large saucepan over a medium-high heat. Add a drizzle of olive oil and fry the onions, garlic, carrots and celery with the spices and salt for 3–4 minutes, stirring. Add the cavolo nero and fry, stirring, until wilted. Add all the remaining ingredients except the beans and the extra virgin olive oil, stir well and simmer for 15 minutes.

Add the beans and a drizzle of extra virgin olive oil, then taste and adjust the seasoning with salt and pepper. Serve hot.

Tip
Serve the ribollita with some good rustic bread, gluten free if required.

VE Opt for agave syrup and rawmesan (see page 28).
GF Omit the bread or opt for gluten-free bread.

*Facing page: Roasted
Baby Pumpkin (page 115).*

Garlic Mushrooms and Cavolo Nero with Red Rice and Fried Eggs

SERVES 4

200g red rice, or other whole grain rice
olive oil, for frying
300g chestnut mushrooms, sliced
4 garlic cloves, minced
150g cavolo nero (black cabbage or kale), stalks removed and finely chopped
a handful of flat-leaf parsley, roughly chopped, plus extra to serve
2 tablespoons nutritional yeast or grated Parmesan, optional
salt and freshly ground black pepper, to taste

TO SERVE:

4 fried medium organic eggs
lemon wedges
2 small avocados, sliced

Rice dishes like risottos and paellas are perfect for big gatherings and small budgets, where you can combine a variety of ingredients with rice to cook conveniently together in one pan. For this dish, you only have to cook the rice ahead in a separate pan, which requires less attention and stirring from you than a risotto or paella. I'm using red rice, which gives a nutty flavour, but you can use other varieties, such as brown, black or basmati. This dish is filling and quick and you can cook the recipe a day ahead.

Cook the rice according to the instructions on the packet (for red rice, around 45 minutes). Set aside.

Add a drizzle of oil to a pan over a high heat and fry the mushrooms, stirring gently, for 2 minutes. Reduce the heat to medium and fry for a further 2–3 minutes or until the excess moisture has reduced. Reserve a few of the prettiest mushrooms for garnish.

Add another drizzle of oil, the garlic and cavolo nero, increase the heat to medium-high again and fry, stirring, for 1–2 minutes until the cabbage is wilted. Return all the remaining main ingredients and stir to mix. Reduce the heat and fry for 2–3 minutes.

Serve garnished with the reserved mushrooms, along with the fried eggs, extra parsley, lemon wedges and avocado slices.

Tip
Serve with a tangy salad.

VE Opt for nutritional yeast; omit the eggs to serve.
GF ✓

Chipotle Jackfruit Tacos

MAKES 8 TACOS/SERVES 4 AS A MAIN
AND 8 AS A STARTER
vegetable oil, for frying
2x 400g cans green (young) jackfruit
  in brine, drained
150ml water or vegetable broth

SPICE MIX:
2 garlic cloves, crushed
1 teaspoon grated fresh ginger or
  ground ginger
2 tablespoons nutritional yeast (optional)
1 tablespoon dried oregano
1 tablespoon chipotle paste
1 teaspoon smoked paprika
1 teaspoon ground cumin
1 teaspoon ground coriander
1 teaspoon ground cinnamon or raw
  cacao powder
¾ teaspoon salt, plus extra to taste
¼ teaspoon freshly ground black pepper
2 tablespoons red wine vinegar
2 tablespoons olive oil

TO SERVE:
8 corn tortillas
lime wedges
nutritonal yeast to sprinkle (optional)
150ml dairy or vegan soured cream
hot sauce, such as Cholula or other
  hot sauces containing jalapeños or
  habanero chillies. Sriracha sauce will
  also do the trick.

TOPPINGS:
Serve with fresh salad toppings of
  your choice, such as chopped or
  sliced avocado, red onion, peppers,
  tomatoes, cucumber, cabbage and
  baby spinach

A great taco offers a variety of textures and flavours, and this easy recipe featuring Spicy Jackfruit ticks all the boxes. The toppings of coriander, avocado and soured cream offer a fresh, cool contrast. Many people enjoy tacos frequently, using ready-made spice mixes. Impress your guests by making your own spice mix - it adds a vibrant homemade flavour that is superior to industrial mixes. These tacos are enhanced with a little kick of chipotle heat - chipotle is a dried and smoky variety of jalapeño pepper. You can substitute the chipotle paste for another chilli.

In a bowl, mix together all the ingredients for the spice mix into a paste. Heat a frying pan over a medium heat. Add a drizzle of vegetable oil and then the spice mix and break it up with a wooden spoon. And the jackfruit and fry, stirring, for 2–3 minutes until it is well coated with the spice mixture. Add water and let the jackfruit simmer and reduce in the spice mix for 20 minutes; if the pan dries out too quickly, add a little more water. Taste and adjust the seasoning with salt, then set aside.

Fill the tortillas with the jackfruit and fresh salad toppings and serve with lime wedges, nutritional yeast, soured cream and hot sauce.

VE Opt for vegan soured cream to serve.
GF Use corn tortillas.

Bibimbap Bowls

SERVES 4

KIMCHI (makes 500g):

500g Chinese cabbage or other sturdy
    cabbage variety

2½ tablespoons salt

1 tablespoons gochugaru or other hot
    chilli paste or sauce

vegetable oil, for frying

4 medium organic eggs

300g cooked rice or quinoa

150g fried shiitake mushrooms

100g kimchi

SAUCE:

1 tablespoon coconut or brown sugar

1 teaspoon grated fresh ginger

1 teaspoon very finely chopped garlic

2 tablespoons water

2 tablespoons shoyu soy or tamari sauce

1 tablespoon toasted sesame oil

TOPPING OPTIONS:

carrot, cucumber and radishes,
    freshly chopped

simple green leaves, such as spinach or
    pak choi

beansprouts

spring onions

kimchi

sprinkles of sesame seeds

This rendition of a traditional everyday Korean dish features cooked rice (or quinoa), shiitake mushrooms and a vibrant array of fresh veggies, all fired up by fermented kimchi. It's easily turned into a festive crowd-pleaser with the addition of eye-catching toppings. The kimchi can be prepared two weeks to a few hours before serving. The longer it sits the more delicious the fermented flavour develops. You can also buy ready-made kimchi from Asian supermarkets or health shops. Choose an organic brand if you can.

First make the kimchi: roughly chop the cabbage and tip into a bowl. Cover with the salt and leave at room temperature for a few hours. Halfway through, toss the cabbage carefully. Rinse the cabbage and squeeze out the excess water with your hands. Mix well with the rest of the kimchi ingredients in the bowl. Allow the flavour to develop for an hour before serving or leave for 24 hours at room temperature and then keep it sealed in a sterilised jar in the fridge for up to two weeks.

Whisk together all the ingredients for the sauce in a jug. Heat up a pan and add a drizzle of vegetable oil. Fry the eggs and set aside until assembly (alternatively serve raw eggs on the hot rice).

To assemble the bibimbap, put the different elements on the table for guests to compose their own bowls or prepare the bowls by adding a serving of the cooked rice or quinoa, fried shiitake mushrooms, kimchi and a fried egg, along with some of the freshly prepared veggies and any other topping choices. Drizzle the sauce over the rice or quinoa and egg.

VE Omit the eggs.

GF Opt for tamari sauce.

Aubergine and Red Pepper Lasagne with Cherry Tomatoes

SERVES 4

600ml Sugo Sauce (see page 143)
1 roasted red pepper from a jar, drained
250g ricotta
250g mascarpone
1 garlic clove, minced with ½ teaspoon
    salt
1 teaspoon lemon juice
4 medium/small aubergines. thinly sliced
olive oil, for brushing
salt and freshly ground black pepper,
    to taste
50g baby spinach or Kale Crisps
    (see page 15)
15g basil
a handful of cherry tomatoes, halved,
    to garnish

This is what I would call a lady lasagne, as it's got loads of flavour but without the heaviness. That's because it's made with aubergine slices instead of the usual pasta sheets, which results in a lighter, altogether juicier dish.

Preheat the oven to 200°C/gas mark 6. Put the sugo sauce and roasted red pepper in a blender or food processor and whizz until smooth. Mix the ricotta and mascarpone or vegan cream cheese with the garlic and lemon juice.

Brush the aubergine slices with olive oil and lightly sprinkle with salt and pepper. Arrange a layer of aubergine slices in the base of an ovenproof dish, then cover with a thin layer of the sugo sauce. Add a layer of spinach or kale and add a handful of basil (reserve a few leaves for the top). Repeat the layers, finishing with a final layer of aubergine slices, and top with the ricotta mixture. Arrange the cherry tomato halves on top, press them down into the ricotta mixture, along with the basil leaves, then season lightly with salt and pepper. Bake for 25 minutes, checking 5 minutes before the end of the baking time to ensure that the lasagne isn't burning. Serve hot with a fresh salad.

Tip
The lasagne can be prepared a day ahead, then cooled and kept, covered, in the fridge. Reheat in the oven preheated to 200°C/gas mark 6 for 10 minutes.

VE Opt for vegan cream cheese instead of the ricotta and mascarpone.
GF ✓

Roasted Ragù and Pappardelle

SERVES 4

olive oil, for drizzling

400g dried pappardelle or pasta of
    your choice

100ml dry white wine

70g Parmesan or rawmesan (see
    page 28), grated, or 2 tablespoons
    nutritional yeast

50g black olives, pitted

1 teaspoon honey or agave syrup

salt and freshly ground black pepper,
    to taste

ROASTED RAGÙ:

olive oil, for drizzling

800g mushrooms, such as shiitake,
    portobello or white button,
    roughly chopped

400g good-quality small tomatoes,
    halved

2 aubergines, trimmed and cut into
    small wedges

1 red pepper, cored, deseeded and cut
    into thick strips

6 shallots, cut into wedges

3 garlic cloves, peeled but left whole

salt, for sprinkling

1 tablespoon freshly ground fennel seeds

1 tablespoon rosemary leaves, chopped,
    or thyme leaves

1 teaspoon dried chilli flakes

TO SERVE:

extra virgin olive oil

basil

grated Parmesan or rawmesan (see
    page 28), or breadcrumbs

Italian food is naturally full of fresh vegetables and this family-style pasta dish features roasted mushrooms, tomatoes and aubergine in a scrumptious ragù, although you can easily vary the vegetables according to your taste or what's in season. Pappardelle gives the dish a rustic quality and soaks up the sauce and herbs for a mouthwatering experience.

To make the roasted ragù, preheat the oven to 200°C/gas mark 6. Line a large baking tray with baking paper.

Arrange all the prepared vegetables (including the garlic) in a single layer on the tray. Drizzle with olive oil and sprinkle with salt and the ground fennel seeds, rosemary and chilli flakes. Roast for 45–55 minutes, checking frequently during the last 20 minutes of roasting time that the veggies aren't burning.

Meanwhile, bring a large pan of water to the boil and add a drizzle of olive oil and a generous pinch of salt. Cook the pappardelle, or other pasta, for 2 minutes less than instructed on the packet. Turn off the heat and drain the pasta, reserving 600ml of the cooking water. Return the pasta to the pan with the reserved cooking water and add a drizzle of olive oil to keep it moist and give it a sheen.

Pick out the roasted garlic cloves from the tray, crush them with a fork and mix with the pasta. Add the remainder of the roasted veggies, the wine, Parmesan or rawmesan or nutritional yeast, the olives and the honey or agave syrup and heat over a medium-high heat. Leave to simmer briskly, stirring gently, for about 2–2½ minutes until the liquid has reduced and been absorbed into the pasta. Taste and adjust the seasoning with salt and pepper, drizzle with extra virgin olive oil and serve sprinkled with basil and extra Parmesan, rawmesan or breadcrumbs.

VE Use egg-free pasta; opt for rawmesan or
nutritional yeast.
GF Use gluten-free pasta, and gluten-free
breadcrumbs, if using, to serve.

Roasted Baby Pumpkins
Stuffed with Harissa Lentils

SERVES 6

3 baby pumpkins or small squashes
olive oil, for brushing
salt, for sprinkling

STUFFING:

200g dried Puy lentils, rinsed
    and drained
50g harissa
2 tablespoons olive oil
40g dried white breadcrumbs or
    panko breadcrumbs
4 shallots, diced
3 garlic cloves, minced
a handful of raisins, finely chopped
leaves from 6 thyme sprigs
1 teaspoon ground cumin
juice of ½ lemon
salt and freshly ground black pepper,
    to taste

ZESTY TAHINI CREAM:

3 tablespoons tahini
50ml olive oil
1 garlic clove
½ teaspoon salt
1 teaspoon honey or agave syrup
2 tablespoons lemon juice

TO SERVE:

mint leaves
a handful of nuts, such as toasted pecans,
    walnuts or almonds
50g feta or goat's cheese, crumbled

When you want to create a show-stopping, full-flavoured beauty of a dish, go for this one, presented in mini pumpkins and squashes as edible serving bowls. This recipe uses a typical North African flavour palette, combining Puy lentils with spicy harissa, raisins, cumin, feta and nuts, drizzled with a zesty tahini cream for a decadent and delicious finish.

Preheat the oven to 190°C/gas mark 5. Halve the pumpkins or squashes horizontally. Spoon out the seeds and membranes, then brush the pumpkins or squashes inside and outside with olive oil and sprinkle with salt. Place the pumpkins or squashes on a baking tray (trim them if needed to stand stable) and roast for 45 minutes.

To prepare the stuffing, bring 1 litre of water to the boil in a saucepan. Add the lentils, reduce the heat and simmer gently for 20–25 minutes until tender. Drain and rinse in cold water. Loosen the harissa with the olive oil to make a smooth sauce. Add to a bowl with the cooked lentils and all the remaining stuffing ingredients and mix together well.

Divide the lentil stuffing between the pumpkin halves and roast for a further 20 minutes.

Meanwhile, mix together the ingredients for the tahini cream. (It can be made a day ahead, sealed and stored in the fridge until 20 minutes before serving.) The pumpkins can be prepared and stuffed a day before serving. Store, covered, in the fridge and roast for 20 minutes before serving.

Serve with fresh mint leaves, a few nuts and crumbled feta cheese and tahini cream.

VE Opt for agave syrup. Use vegan cheese.
GF Use gluten-free breadcrumbs.

Tunisian Aubergine and Pepper Stew with Couscous

SERVES 4

olive oil, for frying

4 shallots, finely chopped

1 red pepper, cored, deseeded and
   sliced in strips

2 garlic cloves, minced

2 medium aubergines, chopped

¾ teaspoon salt, plus extra to taste

400g can chopped tomatoes

4–5 sun-dried tomatoes in oil, drained
   and finely chopped (optional)

juice of ½ lemon

3 dried figs, or other dried fruit,
   finely chopped

400ml vegetable stock

TABIL SPICE MIX:

1½ tablespoons coriander seeds

¾ tablespoon cumin seeds

½ tablespoon caraway seeds

½ teaspoon dried chilli flakes

COUSCOUS:

240g wholegrain couscous or quinoa

420ml boiling hot vegetable stock

YOGURT DRESSING:

200ml Greek or vegan yogurt

a small handful of chopped mint

1 teaspoon honey or agave syrup

salt and freshly ground black pepper,
   to taste

TO SERVE:

a handful of flat-leaf parsley leaves

flatbreads

baby spinach

toasted almonds

orange wedges (optional)

a handful of pomegranate seeds
   (optional)

Tunisian cooking is often overshadowed by the celebrated Moroccan cuisine, but after being introduced to it, I fell in love! Tunisian food is a blend of Mediterranean and North African flavours, and the characteristic spice mix is tabil, widely used on bread and in various warm dishes, and featured in this aubergine one. Here, the aubergine and spices are married together in a tagine-style stew, which is both comforting and exciting, drizzled with a creamy yogurt dressing.

Heat a frying pan over a medium heat and toast the tabil spice mix for about 20–30 seconds only, stirring. Grind in a spice or coffee grinder, or pulse in a blender, to fine granules. Set aside.

Heat a large saucepan over a medium heat. Add a drizzle of olive oil and fry the shallots and red pepper, stirring frequently, for about 5–7 minutes until translucent. Add the garlic, aubergine and tabil spice mix with an extra drizzle of olive oil, then stir to coat the aubergine with the spice. Fry for about 5 minutes until the aubergine is nicely browned. Add the salt, tomatoes, lemon juice, dried figs or other dried fruit and stock, mix together well and then leave the stew to simmer for 15 minutes while you make the couscous or quinoa and yogurt dressing.

Put the couscous or quinoa in a bowl. Pour over the boiling hot stock and leave to soak for 10 minutes. Meanwhile, mix together the ingredients for the yogurt dressing in a bowl.

Taste and adjust the seasoning of the aubergine stew with salt, then serve with the couscous or quinoa, and the flatbreads, pomegranate seeds and spinach salad.

VE Opt for vegan yogurt.

GF Opt for quinoa and gluten-free flatbreads.

6. SIDES AND SHARING DISHES

Side dishes sometimes turn out to be the most exciting component of a meal. So for this chapter I've gathered together some of my all-time favourites that work just as well served as sharing dishes as they do in support of mains. On offer is a mix of those that provide a counterbalance or calming, cooling backdrop to feistier dishes and others that add a powerful injection of concentrated flavour.

It's easy to put together a selection of these dishes to make a great sharing table, from which your guests can pick and mix to create an exciting, varied meal, or combine them with dishes from elsewhere in the book. You can also simply serve them as accompaniments to lead dishes, or on their own as starters.

Crispy Sesame Broccoli

SERVES 8

200g panko breadcrumbs
grated zest of ½ orange
1 teaspoon dried chilli flakes
½ teaspoon salt
olive oil, for drizzling
1kg broccoli, cut down the length with
   the florets
2 tablespoons tahini
2 tablespoons shoyu soy or tamari sauce
1 garlic clove, peeled and crushed

A quick roasting of these broccoli stems gives them a pleasing crunchy bite, and then they are coated in nutty tahini and panko breadcrumbs for extra deliciousness. This works perfectly when contrasted with smooth-textured dishes, such as Tofu Dengaku (see page 125) or Lemongrass and Butternut Squash Soup (see page 139).

Preheat the oven to 220°C/gas mark 7. Line a baking tray with baking paper.

Mix together the panko, orange zest, chilli flakes and salt. Heat a frying pan over a medium heat. Add a little drizzle of olive oil and fry the panko mixture, stirring, for about 3–4 minutes until golden. Transfer to a bowl and set aside.

Toss the broccoli with about 1 tablespoon olive oil in a bowl, then arrange in a single layer, without overlapping, on the lined baking tray. Roast for 8 minutes, then flip the broccoli over and roast for a further 7 minutes. While the broccoli is roasting, mix together the tahini, soy and garlic.

Remove the broccoli from the oven and dip one side of each stalk in the tahini mixture and then in the panko mixture. Place on a platter and sprinkle with the rest of the panko mixture. Serve hot.

VE ✓

GF Use gluten-free breadcrumbs instead of panko; opt for tamari sauce.

Left to right from top: Sambal Goreng Buncis, page 126, Lemongrass and Butternut Squash Soup, page 139, Jackfruit Bulgogi, page 125, Jackfruit Bulgogi Salad, page 89, Tofu Dengaku, page 125.

Jackfruit Bulgogi

The Jacktree bears the biggest fruit in the world and its stringy fleshy texture makes it ideal to use as a savoury addition to salads, breads and stews, This delicious jackfruit bulgogi can be added to salads, like the Asian-style one on page 89. I use canned green jackfruit in brine, which you will easily find in Asian supermarkets or online. It's important that you choose the green jackfruit as the ripe jackfruit is sweet and is best used in dessert.

—

SERVES 4
600g canned green jackfruit, drained
vegetable oil, for frying
water as needed
sesame seeds

MARINADE:
1 tablespoon olive oil
3 tablespoons shoyu soy or tamari sauce
¾ tablespoon gochujang chilli paste or sriracha
1 teaspoon freshly grated ginger
1 garlic clove, crushed
1 tablespoon coconut sugar or agave syrup
1 tablespoon toasted sesame oil
1 teaspoon lemon juice
salt and freshly ground black pepper, to taste

Put the jackfruit in a bowl. Mix the marinade ingredients together and pour over the jackfruit. Massage the jackfruit with your hands, breaking up the bigger pieces and working the marinade into the fruit. Leave to marinate for 10 minutes (or up to 24 hours in the fridge) or fry straight away.

Heat a pan over a medium-high heat, add a drizzle of oil and fry the jackfruit. Add a little water to ensure the jackfruit doesn't dry out too quickly. Continue frying and adding small amounts of water for 15 minutes. Fry for a further 5 minutes without adding water to let the jackfruit dry out. Taste and adjust with salt and pepper. This is delicious served warm, sprinkled with sesame seeds but can also be served cold.

VE ✓

GF Opt for tamari sauce.

Tofu Dengaku

Not everyone loves tofu, but if you're among those, this traditional Japanese recipe is simply irresistible. Tofu is brushed with a miso-based glaze to give its neutral taste a serious boost of flavour and finished under intense dry heat to make it deliciously crisp on the outside.

—

SERVES 6
400g block firm tofu, drained
½ teaspoon sesame seeds
1 spring onion, finely chopped

MISO GLAZE:
4 tablespoons red miso paste (aka miso), or use another miso of your choice
1 tablespoon shoyu soy or tamari sauce
1 tablespoon agave syrup
1½ tablespoons mirin
1½ tablespoons sake
1 tablespoon rice vinegar
1 tablespoon freshly grated ginger

Preheat the oven on the grill setting or to 240°C/gas mark 9 or its highest setting, or preheat the grill to high. Line a baking tray with baking paper.

Lightly press the tofu between sheets of kitchen paper and leave for a few minutes to absorb the excess moisture. Meanwhile, mix together all the ingredients for the miso glaze in a bowl until smooth.

Slice the tofu into equal bite-sized pieces. Heat a frying pan over a high heat and fry the tofu for about 2 minutes on each side until golden brown. Transfer the tofu pieces to the lined tray and brush the miso glaze generously over the top of each. Grill for 3½–4 minutes until dark brown. If your oven doesn't have a fan function, prop the door open slightly to ensure that the tofu doesn't steam in its own moisture.

Transfer the tofu to a plate, insert a cocktail stick into each piece and sprinkle with the sesame seeds and spring onion. It's best served warm, but can be enjoyed after cooling down. The miso glaze can be prepared a day in advance and kept, tightly covered or in an airtight container, in the fridge.

VE ✓

GF Choose a gluten-free miso paste and opt for tamari sauce.

Sambal Goreng Buncis

Sambal goreng buncis is a popular Indonesian dish and one of my favourite ways to eat green beans, cooked with coconut milk, chilli, ginger and garlic. This dish is lovely served with rice, grilled vegetables, eggs, tofu or pickles.

SERVES 4
vegetable oil, for frying
400g green beans, cut into about 5cm lengths
250ml coconut milk
2–3 kaffir lime leaves (optional)

SPICE PASTE:
4 garlic cloves, crushed
1 shallot or small red onion, chopped
1 lemongrass stalk, tough outer layers and stalk top removed, bulb end trimmed and sliced (use only the purple-tinged rings)
1 tablespoon very finely chopped fresh ginger
1 tablespoon ground or finely chopped fresh galangal
2 tablespoons vegetable oil
2 tablespoons shoyu soy or tamari sauce
1 tablespoon coconut sugar
1 tablespoon fresh lime juice
1–3 teaspoons sambal oelek or other hot chilli sauce, such as sriracha, or finely chopped red chilli, to taste
½ teaspoon salt, plus extra to taste

Put all the ingredients for the spice paste in a blender and whizz to a smooth paste.

Heat a large frying pan over a medium heat. Add a drizzle of vegetable oil and fry the spice paste, stirring, for about 1–2 minutes until it starts to dry out. Add the beans and stir-fry until they are thoroughly covered with the spice paste. Add the coconut milk and bring to the boil, then reduce the heat to a simmer. Add the kaffir lime leaves, if using, and cook the beans for about 15 minutes or until they are tender but still have some bite – the exact cooking time will depend on the type and thickness of the beans, but it's usually 10–20 minutes. Remove the kaffir lime leaves. Taste and adjust the seasoning with salt. Serve warm.

VE ✓ GF Opt for tamari sauce.

Seared Miso Mushrooms

Flavoured with miso, these mushrooms are pure umami bombs, adding a powerful flavour hit wherever they are used and making any vegetarian dish truly mouthwatering. I've chosen oyster mushrooms here, which are more delicate than the fleshy shiitake.

SERVES 4
25g red miso paste (aka miso)
25g ghee, butter or vegetable oil, plus extra for frying
250g oyster mushrooms

Mix the miso with the ghee, butter or vegetable oil until smooth. Heat a frying pan to a high heat. Add a little ghee, butter or vegetable oil and fry the oyster mushrooms for 2 minutes without stirring. Then fry, stirring, for a further 2 minutes. Add the miso mixture and fry, stirring, for a final minute. Serve warm as a side dish.

VE Opt for vegetable oil.
GF Use a dark miso paste instead of red but check the contents to ensure that it's gluten free.

Tsukemono

Historically, pickling was used as a way of preserving vegetables and fruit over the winter. Although it's still a useful method for extending the shelf life of foods, the major win with pickling is the amazing flavours that result. Pickles add interest and finish to dishes, but there is much more to pickles than the little gherkins we are used to, in particular tsukemono, the prince of pickles. Delicately flavoured, these Japanese pickles provide a striking contrast to fresh, light food such as steamed dishes and cooked rice.

Use this brine juice to pickle any fresh vegetables you like, and serve them in stews, salads, breads or to top canapés.

———

MAKES 500G PICKLES
500g vegetables of your choice, such as cucumber, shallots, courgette, turnips, radishes, daikon and/or carrots, peeled as appropriate and thinly sliced or cut into matchsticks

BRINE JUICE:
250ml umesu vinegar or shoyu soy or tamari sauce
250ml rice vinegar

OPTIONAL BRINE ADD-INS:
a small amount of wasabi
thinly sliced ginger
red shiso seasoning

Mix the ingredients for the brine juice together in a glass measuring jug. Put the prepared veggies in one large or two smaller sterilised jars. Pour over the brine juice to cover and seal the jar(s). Leave to pickle in the fridge for three days before serving. Once opened, use the pickles within 3–4 days. The pickles will keep, unopened, in the fridge for up to 2 weeks, if a sterile jar is used.

VE ✓
GF Opt for tamari sauce.

Tip
Umesu vinegar colours the veg less than either soy and tamari sauces, so for the brighter-coloured pickles, opt for that.

Wakame Salad

If you are looking for an easy way to enjoy sea vegetables, look no further. In fact, I recommend that you flag this page in the book because this recipe is phenomenal in so many ways. As well as serving it as a salad, you can add it to Asian rice bowls and soups, serve it with eggs and avocados or use it as a sandwich filling with fresh potatoes and egg salad or topping. It's also great served as a side with Scandinavian-style dishes, as Japanese and Nordic flavours marry perfectly.

———

SERVES 4
20g dried wakame

DRESSING:
2 tablespoons rice vinegar
2 tablespoons light soy or tamari sauce
2 teaspoons sesame seeds
1 teaspoon shichimi togarashi or dried chilli flakes, or more, to taste
1 teaspoon sugar

Soak the wakame in a bowl of warm water for 10–20 minutes. Meanwhile, bring a saucepan of water to the boil. Drain the wakame and blanch in the boiling water for 30 seconds. Immediately drain into a sieve and rinse in ice-cold water. Drain thoroughly and pat with a clean tea towel to absorb the excess moisture. Chop the wakame and transfer to a serving bowl.

Mix together all the ingredients for the dressing in a small bowl, pour over the wakame and serve.

The salad can be kept, tightly covered or in an airtight container, in the fridge for 2–3 days.

VE ✓
GF Opt for tamari sauce.

Baby Pak Choi with Ginger and Garlic

Pak choi is one of my most-loved cabbages! Smooth and crunchy at the same time, it's simply delicious and so easy to cook. There is very little fuss involved in preparing this dish – it's the quality of the ingredients that makes all the difference. This goes well with the Seared Miso Mushrooms (see page 126) and rice dishes.

SERVES 4
4 pak choi
1 tablespoon sesame oil
1 garlic clove, crushed
1 teaspoon freshly grated ginger
2 tablespoons shoyu soy or tamari sauce
75ml water
2 tablespoons sesame seeds

Cut the pak choi lengthways into wedges, keeping the root intact so that the leaves stay together.

Heat a large deep frying pan or wok that has a lid over a medium-high heat. Add the sesame oil, garlic, ginger and soy or tamari sauce and stir briefly to combine. Add the water and pak choi, cover the pan with the lid and leave to steam for 2 minutes.

Remove from the heat and sprinkle with the sesame seeds. Serve warm.

VE ✓
GF Opt for tamari sauce.

Cherry Chutney and Radicchio with Toasted Almonds

Chutney is a smart short cut to maximising flavour, great for using with quality salad and other vegetables to create standout dishes. Here, a few spoonfuls of concentrated chutney are enough to transform radicchio leaves into a scrumptous warm salad. This is ideal for serving as a side dish with curries.

You can use other fruit or berries or vegetables in place of cherries for the chutney.

To make the chutney, heat a frying pan over a medium-high heat. Add a drizzle of olive oil or a little ghee and fry the shallots, ginger, garlic, chilli, spices, fennel seeds and seasoning with the sugar, stirring frequently, for 5–7 minutes or until the shallots are translucent. Add the cherries and red vinegar, reduce the heat and leave the chutney to simmer, stirring, for about 25–30 minutes under a lid, stirring occasionally until the liquid has reduced and the consistency is thick.

Transfer the chutney to a sterilised airtight jar and leave it to cool. Seal the jar and keep in the fridge until you are ready to use. Use the chutney within 2 weeks in the fridge.

To prepare the salad, heat a frying pan over a medium heat. Add a drizzle of vegetable oil and then the chutney, and break it up with a wooden spoon. Add the radicchio and fry for 2–3 minutes, stirring and tossing the leaves to coat with the chutney. Taste and adjust the seasoning with salt and pepper. Sprinkle with toasted almonds and serve.

VE Opt for olive oil.
GF ✓

Tip
Make this a filling main salad dish by adding delicate green salad leaves, avocado, sautéed mushrooms and cooked grains. Dilute the chutney with olive oil and vinegar or lemon juice to use as a dressing.

CHERRY CHUTNEY (MAKES 350–400G):

olive oil or ghee, for frying
4 shallots, thinly sliced
2 teaspoons freshly grated ginger
2 garlic cloves, crushed
1 red chilli, deseeded and finely chopped
1 teaspoon ground cardamom
1 teaspoon ground cinnamon
½ teaspoon fennel seeds
¼ teaspoon freshly ground black pepper
salt, to taste
2 tablespoons coconut sugar or brown sugar
200g pitted cherries
100ml red wine vinegar

CHERRY CHUTNEY RADICCHIO SALAD:
vegetable oil, for frying
2–3 tablespoons Cherry Chutney (see left)
150g radicchio leaves (or other sturdy salad leaves), torn into pieces
salt and freshly ground black pepper, to taste
toasted almonds (or other nuts), roughly chopped, for sprinkling

Labneh and Harissa-roasted Carrots with Mint and Almonds

SERVES 4

LABNEH:
500ml full-fat Greek yogurt
150ml good-quality extra virgin olive oil
a handful of mixed herbs, such as mint,
    flat-leaf parsley and chives
1 teaspoon finely grated lemon zest
salt and freshly ground black pepper,
    to taste

HARISSA ROASTED CARROTS:
400g baby carrots or carrots,
    halved lengthways
100ml olive oil
2 tablespoons harissa
salt, to taste

TO SERVE:
crumbled toasted almonds
fresh mint leaves
extra virgin olive oil
salt and freshly ground balck pepper,
    to taste
sprinkles of sumac (optional)

Contrasting flavours make powerful combinations. In this sharing dish, harissa, a chilli paste full of slow-roasted hot pepper flavour spices up humble carrots, paired against a cool labneh. It's easy to make your own labneh, a soft cheese made from strained yogurt. It needs at least a few days in the fridge before it's ready; you can use shop-bought labneh instead if time is in short supply. It's available from Middle Eastern supermarkets and many well-stocked Western supermarkets and delis.

To make the labneh, line a sieve with a muslin cloth and place over a large bowl. Put the yogurt in the muslin, then gather up the cloth edges and twist together. Leave the yogurt to drain over the bowl in the fridge for three days.

Discard the liquid in the bowl. Shape the yogurt, which will have thickened into a fresh cheese, into balls and place in a deep bowl or sterilised jar. Mix together the extra virgin olive oil, herbs, lemon zest and salt and pepper to taste and pour the mixture over the labneh. Cover the bowl tightly or seal the jar and leave the labneh to marinate in the fridge for a day or up to a week.

To make the harissa-roasted carrots, preheat the oven to 200°C/gas mark 6. Line a baking tray with baking paper. Mix together the olive oil and harissa in a bowl. Add the carrots with salt to taste and toss to coat with the harissa mixture. Spread the carrots on the lined tray and roast for 40 minutes, keeping an eye on the tray for the last 10 minutes to avoid burning.

To serve, spread the labneh on a plate and top the labneh with harissa-roasted carrots and toasted almonds and fresh mint leaves, drizzle with extra virgin olive oil and sprinkle salt, pepper and sumac, if using.

VE Opt for vegan soft cheese, and olive oil for frying.
GF ✓

Tip
Labneh is often served with hummus (see page 34). It can also be whipped and used as as tangy butter cream on cakes (see Chai Carrot Cake on page 186, just omit the herbs and add 2 teaspoons honey or agave syrup) or served plain, drizzled with honey or syrup and sprinkled with typical Middle Eastern toppings such as nuts, pomegranate seeds, warming spices such as cinnamon or cardamom, or with preserved or fresh fruit.

The Big Roast!

SERVES 8

1 medium butternut squash, halved
    lengthways, seeds and membrane
    removed, peeled and sliced
    into wedges

6 beetroots, peeled and cut into wedges

2 red peppers, cored, deseeded and cut
    into thick strips

12 carrots, peeled and cut into
    chunky pieces

4 red onions, cut into wedges

extra virgin olive oil, for drizzling

5 sage leaves, finely shopped

leaves picked from 4 thyme sprigs

salt, to taste

sprinkling of dried chilli flakes, to taste

50g toasted pumpkin seeds

YOGURT LEMON GARLIC SAUCE:

200ml yogurt or coconut yogurt

1 teaspoon lemon juice

1 garlic clove, crushed in ¾ teaspoon salt

1 teaspoon honey or agave syrup

I made this huge roast for my beloved family for one of the first dinners I hosted in my home. I wanted to make a vegetarian meal that they would all love, and this great big colourful tray of roasted veggies did the job perfectly. It's a very easy recipe where butternut squash, beetroot, carrots, peppers and onions are roasted together with sage and thyme, then drizzled with a cool lemon-flavoured yogurt sauce. Serve with couscous, any grain or fresh bread.

Preheat the oven to 220°C/gas mark 7. Line two large baking trays with baking paper. Mix together all the ingredients for the yogurt lemon garlic sauce in a bowl and set aside until ready to serve.

Put the prepared veggies in a large bowl, drizzle with olive oil, sprinkle with the herbs and season to taste with salt and chilli flakes. Toss to coat and then arrange the vegetables in a single layer, without overlapping, on the lined baking trays. Roast for 45 minutes or until the veggies are tender. Serve the roasted veggies hot, spinkle with toasted pumpkin seeds and serve with the yogurt sauce.

Tip

The roast can be varied with the seasons, using other root vegetables and different squashes in the recipe.

VE Use vegan yogurt; opt for agave syrup.
GF ✓

Potatoes Serundeng

Serundeng is a seasoning of spice-tempered coconut flakes often used to liven up rice and curries in Indonesia. It's utterly delicious. I use serundeng on a variety of foods, and here I'm transforming potatoes with it. Serve with curries or a fresh salad. Try sprinkling serundeng on roasted vegetables or roots.

SERVES 4
800g quality firm potatoes
salt, to taste
vegetable oil or butter

SERUNDENG (MAKES ABOUT 500G):
500g dessicated coconut
100g coconut sugar
1 teaspoon ground cumin
3 garlic cloves, crushed
1 teaspoon freshly grated ginger
1 teaspoon ground coriander
½ teaspoon salt
200g roasted peanuts, crushed

Boil the potatoes for 15–20 minutes, check doneness after 15 minutes and cook until the potato is soft. Drain and set aside.

Meanwhile, make the serundeng. Heat a frying pan to medium hot. Fry the coconut while continously stirring until the coconut is a deep golden colour, about 2–3 minutes. Add the sugar, spices and salt and continue stirring to mix well. Add the peanuts and stir, then remove from the heat. Toss the potato with oil or butter and sprinkle generously with serundeng. Serve warm.

Tip
Keep the remainder of the serundeng stored sealed in a cool place.

VE ✓ GF ✓

Roasted Parsnip Fries with Ajvar Dip

Parsnips are an underrated root veg that deserves more attention. It's best flavour comes out when roasted. Use as a side dish, where you normally would use potatoes, sweet potatoes or rice. Here I paired it with a hungarian red pepper dip, Ajvar – a delicious dip that can be used with breads, salads and pizzas too.

SERVES 4
AJVAR DIP:
1 aubergine, halved
4 red peppers, cut into pieces
5 garlic cloves
50ml olive oil
1 teaspoon lemon juice
1 teaspoon agave syrup or honey
salt and pepper, to taste

6 parsnips, cut into strips or wedges
olive oil
1 tablespoon rosemary or thyme (fresh and chopped or dried)
salt

Preheat the oven to 220°C/gas mark 7. Line a baking tray with baking paper. For the ajvar dip, place the aubergine, red peppers and garlic on an oven tray and roast in the oven for 10 minutes. Remove the garlic and roast the remaning ingredients for another 30 minutes. Let them cool, transfer to a food processor and blend with the rest of the ajvar ingredients. Taste and adjust with salt and pepper. Toss the parsnip with the herbs and oil in a bowl and spread out in a single layer on the lined tray. Roast for 25–30 minutes. Serve warm as a side or as a small bite with the ajvar or another dip (like the Artichoke dip on page 34).

VE Opt for agave syrup. GF ✓

Best Tomato Salad Ever

Tomato salads work wonders as a side with savoury dishes, but there's a well-known 'secret' that makes all the difference between a bland and a magnificent tomato salad. If you marinate the tomatoes in a sour liquid (lemon in the summer and vinegar in the winter), garlic, salt and a sweetener (if you are using balsamic vingar use less) you get the most wonderful and delicious tomato salad. Serve it just as it is or include as many add-ons as you like.

SERVES 4
400g quality tomatoes, chopped or sliced
100ml vinegar or lemon juice
2 garlic cloves, crushed in ¾ teaspoon salt
2 teaspoons honey or agave syrup
100ml extra virgin olive oil

OPTIONAL ADD-ONS
1 red onion, minced or thinly sliced
fresh green leaves such as baby spinach or rocket
fresh herbs, such as basil or parsley
mozzarella, feta cheese or vegan cheese

Mix the tomato and the marinade ingredients in a bowl, taste and adjust the flavour with salt or your sweetener. Leave to marinate for 30 minutes to 2 hours. You can choose to drain the liquid or keep it in the salad as a dressing. Include any add-ons if you like a fuller salad.

VE Opt for vegan cheese and agave syrup.
GF ✓

Kimchi Fried Rice

Rice can easily become the main attraction on the table, just fry it with kimchi and it will be both exciting and hot! Use the kimchi on page 109 or shop-bought, but make sure it's good quality.

SERVES 4

3 tablespoons kimchi (see page 109)
2 tablespoons shoyu soy or tamari sauce
sesame oil or other vegetable oil, for frying
600g cooked brown rice
a handful of fresh herbs like coriander or parsley, or baby spinach

Blend the kimchi with the sauce and 1 tablespoon sesame oil. In a bowl mix the rice and the kimchi mixture.

Heat a pan over a medium-high heat, add the rice and cook for 4 minutes. Taste and adjust, adding kimchi juice or soy sauce if needed. Lower the temperature and let the rice fry for a further 2 minutes, while stirring. Serve warm and mixed with fresh herbs.

VE ✓
GF Opt for tamari sauce.

Rainbow Noodles with Coriander Pesto

This is an incredibly juicy and fresh option to noodles, pasta and rice. Spiralise rainbow carrots, courgette, daikon and other suitable vegetables and serve with a pesto made of coriander, lime, garlic, ginger, sesame oil and chilli.

SERVES 4

CORIANDER PESTO:
50g fresh coriander
100ml olive oil, and extra to taste
2 tablespoons toasted sesame oil
50g roasted cashew nuts or other nuts
juice of 1 lime or 2 tablespoons lemon juice
1 tablespoon nutritional yeast or finely grated Parmesan (optional)
salt, to taste

800g vegetables such as rainbow carrots, courgette or daikon, peeled and spiralised

Blend the pesto ingredients into a smooth paste. Add a little extra water if you want a looser consistency. Serve the pesto with spiralised veggies or use as a condiment with savoury dishes.

VE Opt for nutritional yeast.
GF Opt for tamari sauce.

Lemongrass and Butternut Squash Soup

This warming and vibrant soup balances comforting butternut with lively lemongrass and chilli. Serve with fresh salads or rice dishes.

SERVES 4

2 butternut squash, halved lengthways and the seeds and membrane removed
olive oil
salt
4 shallots, roughly chopped
2 garlic cloves, crushed
400ml vegetable broth
400ml coconut milk
2 tablespoons puréed lemongrass
1½ teaspoons gochujang, sriracha or other red chilli paste, and extra to taste
1 teaspoon freshly grated ginger
¾ teaspoon salt

Preheat the oven to 220°C/gas mark 7. Brush the butternut squash with oil and sprinkle with salt. Roast in the middle of the oven, cut-side up, for 1 hour. Scoop out the flesh and transfer the flesh with the shallots and garlic to a food processor. Blend into a smooth purée.

Add the purée to a saucepan, along with the rest of the soup ingredients. Bring to a boil and lower the heat. Allow to simmer for 2–3 minutes. Taste and adjust with salt, if needed

VE ✓
GF ✓

7. AL FRESCO

You can serve many of the dishes in this book outdoors or take them to
pot-luck gatherings, but the ones in this chapter are extra delicious enjoyed in the open air
or particularly portable for bringing with you to a barbecue or on a picnic. One popular choice
for a fun and flexible al fresco cooking and dining experience is pizza, and here are lots of
exciting ideas for topping combinations, together with a recipe for a delicious cauliflower
crust as a gluten-free alternative to a spelt and wheat flour dough base.
There is something irresistible about chargrilling food and eating it outside, so I've
included options for barbecue parties, such as crowd-pleasing Mediterranean-style halloumi
and vegetable skewers complete with grilled pitta breads and a creamy red pepper sauce.
But nothing could be more perfect for a bring-your-own get-together than
a beautiful layered green crêpe cake.

Tahini and Sweet Potato
and Avocado Pizza
page 144.

Tip
It's no problem if you don't have access to an outdoor
pizza oven, as you can cook the pizzas on a hot
charcoal or gas barbecue, or of course pop them into a
regular kitchen oven.

Bake-your-own Pizza Party

MAKES 4 MEDIUM OR 8 SMALL PIZZAS
OR FLATBREADS

BASIC SPELT DOUGH
4 teaspoons fast-action dried yeast
325ml warm (not hot) water
2 tablespoons honey or agave syrup
600g wholemeal spelt flour, plus extra
    for dusting
400g plain flour or spelt flour
4 teaspoons fine salt
250ml olive oil, plus extra for oiling
semolina flour, for dusting the lined
    baking tray (optional)

SUGO SAUCE
    (MAKES 800ML):
olive oil, for frying
2 shallots, chopped
3 garlic cloves, crushed with 1 teaspoon
    fine salt
2 x 400g cans good-quality plum tomatoes
a handful of basil, chopped
2 tablespoons mixed dried Italian herbs,
    such as oregano, basil and thyme
    (optional)
1 teaspoon honey or agave syrup, or more
    to taste
salt and freshly ground black pepper,
    to taste

CLASSIC TOPPINGS:
Sugo, mozzarella, garlic, herbs, salt and
    freshly ground black pepper

SUGGESTED TOPPING OPTIONS:
peppers, courgette, aubergine, kale,
    spinach, onions, olives, mushrooms,
    fennel, broccoli, sweet potato, nuts
    and seeds, pesto

VE Opt for agave syrup for the spelt dough and
sugo; opt for vegan alternatives to dairy such as
vegan cheese for the topping.
GF The dough is not gluten free.

For a family gathering, this pizza-party formula works like a charm. We have a wood-fired stone pizza oven in the corner of the garden, so pizza has become an outdoor meal for us, and the smell of burnt wood and freshly baked pizzas in the fresh air is heavenly. The key concept here is for your guests to simply create their own pizzas, with a portion of the dough that you have pre-prepared (kids will love it especially!) choosing from a variety of toppings that you provide. The thin spelt pizza base is delicious, and can also be used to make flatbreads.

To make the spelt dough, mix the yeast with the warm water and honey or agave syrup in a small bowl. Leave to stand for about 10 minutes to allow the yeast to activate – it should become foamy on the surface.

Put the flours in a mixing bowl, or in the bowl of a stand mixer fitted with the dough hook, sift over the salt and mix together well. If mixing by hand, make a well in the flour, pour in the yeast mixture and gradually mix in the flour with a fork, then slowly add the olive oil and work into the dough with your hands. Knead the dough on a floured work surface for a few minutes until smooth and elastic. If using a stand mixer, add the yeast mixture with the motor running until incorporated, then slowly pour in the olive oil and continue kneading until the dough is smooth.

Oil a large bowl, add the dough and cover with a clean tea towel. Leave to rise in the kitchen for 1½ hours. Punch the dough down to deflate it and place it on a floured work surface. Divide the dough into four or eight pieces and knead each piece lightly into a ball.

To make the sugo, heat a frying pan over a medium heat. Add a drizzle of olive oil and fry the shallots with the garlic, stirring, for 7–8 minutes until soft. Add all the remaining ingredients and simmer for 15 minutes, stirring occasionally to avoid burning. Add a little water or stock if the sauce dries out too much. Taste and adjust the flavour balance with salt, pepper and honey or agave syrup.

To make the pizzas, lay a sheet of baking paper on a baking tray and sprinkle with a little semolina flour – this is optional, but it adds a delicious texture. Roll out one dough ball with a rolling pin into a thin round – it should be only a few millimetres thick. Add your choice of toppings and transfer to the prepared tray. Repeat with the remainder of the dough balls.

Baking times vary between different methods and ovens: if using an indoor oven, preheat to 220°C/gas mark 7 and bake for 10–18 minutes until the pizza base and toppings are golden and well done. If using a barbecue, place the pizza on the lined baking tray on the metal rack over the fire and bake until it is well done – the time will vary depending on the heat of your barbecue. If using a wood-fired stone pizza oven, start a fire in the oven 2 hours ahead of baking, keep adding wood to build up the heat and loosely close with a lid. Bake the pizza for 1–3 minutes. Overleaf are some suggestions for toppings.

Goat's Cheese and Beetroot Pizza

MAKES 1 PIZZA

¼ quantity of Basic Spelt Dough (see page 143)
olive oil, for drizzling
leaves from 2 sprigs of thyme
100g soft goat's or vegan cheese, crumbled
½ medium beetroot, cooked or raw, peeled and thinly sliced
1 tablespoon thinly sliced raw red onion
salt and freshly ground black pepper, to taste

Roll out the dough into a thin round following the instructions on page 143. Drizzle with olive oil and sprinkle with salt and pepper to taste and the thyme.

Top with the goat's or vegan cheese and then the remaining toppings. Bake following the instructions on page 143.

VE Opt for vegan soft cheese.
GF The dough is not gluten free.

Kale and Mushroom Pizza

MAKES 1 PIZZA

¼ quantity of Basic Spelt Dough (see page 143)
olive oil, for drizzling
a sprinkle of chopped marjoram
a handful of kale leaves (stalks removed), chopped
1 garlic clove, crushed
150g burrata, sliced or torn, or vegan soft cheese
a handful of sliced mushrooms
dried chilli flakes, for sprinkling
grated Parmesan or rawmesan (see page 28), for sprinkling
salt and freshly ground black pepper, to taste

Roll out the dough into a thin round following the instructions on page 143. Drizzle with olive oil and sprinkle with salt and pepper and marjoram.

Put the kale in a bowl with the garlic, and a drizzle of olive oil and massage together with your hands.

Top the pizza with the burrata or vegan cheese and kale, add the mushroom slices and sprinkle with chilli flakes. Bake following the instructions on page 143, then sprinkle with Parmesan or rawmesan and salt before serving.

VE Opt for vegan cheese.
GF The dough is not gluten free.

Tahini, Sweet Potato and Avocado Pizza

MAKES 1 PIZZA

¼ quantity of Basic Spelt Dough (see page 143)
olive oil, for drizzling
pinch of dried chilli flakes
3–4 tablespoons Sugo (see page 143)
1 roasted red pepper from a jar, drained or fresh red pepper, sliced
a handful of fresh spinach
50g sweet potato wedges, precooked
1 tablespoons pine nuts or other nuts
½ avocado, sliced
salt and freshly ground black pepper, to taste

TAHINI SAUCE:
2 tablespoons tahini
1 garlic clove, crushed
3 tablespoons fresh coriander, chopped
100ml water
50ml olive oil
50ml lemon juice
1 teaspoon honey or agave syrup
salt, to taste

Roll out the dough into a thin round following the instructions on page 143. Drizzle with olive oil and sprinkle with salt and pepper and the chilli flakes.

Put the sugo and roasted red pepper in a blender or food processor and whizz until smooth – this is delicious with the tahini. Spread on top of the pizza base, add the spinach and sweet potato wedges and sprinkle over the crushed almonds. Bake following the instructions on page 143.

Meanwhile, whizz together all the ingredients for the tahini sauce with a hand blender in a jug until well blended.

Top the baked pizza with the avocado slices and drizzle over the tahini sauce before serving.

VE Opt for agave syrup for the sauce.
GF The dough is not gluten free.

Broccoli and Pesto Pizza

MAKES 1 PIZZA
¼ quantity of Basic Spelt Dough (see page 143)
olive oil, for drizzling
salt and freshly ground black pepper, to taste
pinch of dried chilli flakes
2 tablespoons pesto
½ garlic clove, crushed
a handful of broccoli raab (rapini or cima di rapa) or broccoli, chopped
75g mozzarella, torn or sliced, or vegan cheese

—

Roll out the dough into a thin round following the instructions on page 143. Drizzle with olive oil and sprinkle with salt and pepper and the chilli flakes. Spread the pizza base with the pesto and garlic, then top with the broccoli raab or broccoli and mozzarella or vegan cheese. Bake following the instructions on page 143.

Tip
You can replace the broccoli raab or broccoli with asparagus, green beans or other green vegetables.

VE Opt for vegan cheese and use vegan pesto.
GF The dough is not gluten free.

Salad in a Jar

Packing your salad in a jar isn't just a brilliant lunch option – it's also a delicious, portable solution when you are asked to bring your own food to a party. This jar is layered with cooked grains, tahini sauce and yogurt, grilled vegetables and fresh salad vegetables and herbs, plant protein in the form of chickpeas and some seeds and nuts for a pleasing crunch.

—

SERVES 1
150g mixed vegetables, such as red pepper, cored and deseeded, aubergine and courgette, chopped
olive oil, for grilling
1 tablespoon harissa
salt, to taste
extra virgin olive oil, for drizzling
1 tablespoon lemon juice
75g cooked freekeh, bulgur wheat, couscous or brown rice
100ml Tahini Sauce (see page 144)
50g labneh or yogurt
50g cherry tomatoes, chopped
50g cucumber, chopped
a handful of mixed herbs, such as flat-leaf parsley and coriander
1 small red onion, thinly sliced
100g drained canned or jarred chickpeas
a handful of baby spinach
a small handful of seeds and nuts – I use hemps seeds and toasted almonds

VE Opt for vegan yogurt.
GF Use a gluten-free grain such as buckwheat or brown rice.

Preheat the oven to 180°C/gas mark 4. Line a baking tray with baking paper.

Put the mixed vegetables in a bowl, drizzle with olive oil and the harissa and toss to coat. Arrange on the lined baking tray in a single layer, season lightly with salt and bake for 50 minutes, flipping the vegetables over halfway through. Remove from the oven and leave to cool. Drizzle with extra olive oil and the lemon juice, then taste and adjust the seasoning with salt.

You will need a clean preserving jar or screw-top jar about 500g in capacity. Layer the ingredients in the jar, starting with the cooked grains. Top with the tahini sauce and labneh or yogurt, then the grilled vegetables, followed by the tomatoes, cucumber, herbs, onion and chickpeas. Finish with the spinach and the seeds and nuts. Seal the jar and keep in the fridge until it's time to leave for your party. It will keep for a day in the fridge.

Cauliflower Crust Pizza with Mozzarella, Spinach and Egg

MAKES 1 PIZZA

CAULIFLOWER CRUST:
150g cauliflower, broken into florets
40g Parmesan or rawmesan (see page 28), finely grated
100g almond or rice or other gluten-free flour
½ teaspoon dried oregano
½ teaspoon dried chilli flakes
½ teaspoon salt
1 medium organic egg

TOPPINGS:
a handful of baby spinach leaves
150g mozzarella, torn or sliced or vegan soft cheese
1 medium organic egg

TO SERVE:
pickled or raw red onion
fresh basil leaves
salt and freshly ground black pepper, to taste
extra virgin olive oil

Yes, you can also make a pizza base with vegetables, and it's delicious! Here I've used cauliflower for a gluten-free alternative to the spelt and wheat pizza dough, which I've topped with creamy mozzarella, spinach and egg. I prefer to bake this in a kitchen oven because the temperature is more controlable for prebaking the pizza base. But you can use an outdoor wood-fired stone pizza oven, as long as you keep a very close eye on it to avoid burning.

If using a wood-fire oven, light a fire in 2 hours before baking. If using an indoor oven, preheat the oven to 250°C/gas mark 9 or its highest setting. Lay a sheet of baking paper on a baking tray.

Put the cauliflower in a food processor and whizz until it is finely ground. Transfer to a mixing bowl, add all the remaining crust ingredients and mix together into a dough.

Flatten and press the dough into a round on the lined baking tray. Bake for 10 minutes if using an indoor oven. If using an outdoor stone pizza oven, bake for a maximum of 1 minute or until the crust has firmed. Remove from the oven, add the spinach, then the mozzarella and finally the egg. Salt and pepper lightly. Bake for a further 30–40 seconds until the egg is firm. If using an indoor oven, bake until the egg has firmed. Remove from the oven and sprinkle with pickled red onion, basil and salt and pepper to taste, then drizzle with extra virgin olive oil.

VE Opt for rawmesan (see page 28) and vegan egg replacer for the pizza base; opt for vegan cheese for topping and omit the egg.
GF ✓

Making homemade gluten-free flour
Buying a bag of nut, seed or oat flour is pricy compared to buying the ingredient whole and grinding it yourself at home. So, simply use a coffee grinder or a powerful blender to grind your chosen nuts, seeds or oats for 20 seconds or until they are finely ground, but be careful not to overgrind, otherwise they will turn into a buttery paste!

Halloumi Veggie Skewers with a Watermelon and Buckwheat Salad

SERVES 4

WATERMELON AND BUCKWHEAT SALAD
100g buckwheat
500ml water
100g baby spinach or rocket
1 red onion, sliced
200g watermelon, diced
100g tomatillos or cherry tomatoes, halved
2 tablespoons fresh finely chopped herbs, such as coriander, parsley or mint
2 tablespoons lemon juice
2 tablespoons extra virgin olive oil
salt, to taste

HALLOUMI VEGGIE SKEWERS:
300g halloumi cheese or mushrooms, cut into bite-sized pieces
8 small or 2 medium red or yellow peppers, cored, deseeded and cut into bite-sized pieces
4 small red onions, cut into bite-sized pieces
2 green tomatillos (or substitute yellow tomatoes if you can't source)
200g cauliflower florets
8 radishes
olive oil, for drizzling
salt and freshly ground black pepper, to taste

CREAMY RED PEPPER SAUCE:
½ red chilli, chopped
2 roasted red peppers from a jar, drained
2 garlic cloves, chopped
100g walnuts
50ml water
2 tablespoons extra virgin olive oil
juice of 1 lime
1 teaspoon honey or agave syrup
salt and freshly ground black pepper, to taste

One of the easiest ways of cooking vegetables on the barbecue is to thread them onto skewers – ideal for preparing at home and transporting to a barbecue party. I love to combine a mix of vegetables with something powerfully savoury in flavour such as halloumi cheese or mushrooms. Serve these skewers with creamy red pepper sauce and a refreshing Watermelon and Buckwheat Salad. Naturally, you can vary the skewered vegetables based on season and availabilty.

Cook the buckwheat in the water for 10 minutes. Put all the ingredients for the creamy red pepper sauce in a blender or food processor and whizz until smooth. Transfer to a bowl and cover tightly or put in an airtight container and refrigerate until ready to serve. Mix the ingredients for the salad in a bowl and set aside until serving.

Put the halloumi or mushrooms with the prepared vegetables in a bowl, drizzle with olive oil and sprinkle with salt and pepper to taste, then toss to coat. Thread the halloumi or mushrooms onto skewers, alternating with the vegetables.

When the coals of your charcoal barbecue have burnt down or your gas barbecue is hot, place the skewers on the metal rack and grill for a few minutes, turning frequently, until charred on all sides. Serve the skewers with the Watermelon Buckwheat Salad and creamy red pepper sauce.

VE Opt for mushrooms for the skewers, vegan crème fraîche for the soured cream and agave syrup for the salsa verde.
GF ✓

Aubergine Kebab with Rainbow Salad, Garlic Sauce, Hummus and Flatbreads

2 medium aubergines, cut into chunks

MARINADE:

2 tablespoons olive oil

1 teaspoon lemon juice

2 teaspoons ground cumin

1 teaspoon ground coriander

1 teaspoon dried chilli flakes

1 teaspoon ground cinnamon

¾ teaspoon salt

GARLIC SAUCE:

100ml olive oil

5 garlic cloves, crushed

2 tablespoons plain yogurt

1 teaspoon agave syrup or honey

¾ teaspoon salt, or more to taste

RAINBOW SALAD

2 avocados, diced

1 small red onion, thinly sliced

100g red or white cabbage, shredded

100g cherry tomatoes, halved

1 red pepper, cut into strips

50g baby spinach

a handful of flat-leaf parsley and mint
 leaves, roughly chopped

a handful of toasted almonds or
 other nuts

TO SERVE:

4 flatbreads

Classic Hummus (see page 34)

harissa

lemon wedges, for squeezing

Yottam Ottolenghi once told me that the best flavours are the bold and simple ones that you find in street food, such as from kebab stalls, and so that's where many culinary stars go to eat. I don't need convincing because I already love pitta bread stuffed with falafel and garlic sauces. As a variation on that theme, here we have aubergines grilled on skewers, marinated in spices such as cumin, ground coriander and chilli to give them a scrumptious flavour, and served with a refreshing minty cucumber salad. You can skip the bread and serve the dish in bowls, and also vary the veggies for grilling.

To prepare the kebabs, mix together all the ingredients for the marinade in a small bowl. Put the aubergines in a bowl, pour over the marinade and toss to coat. Leave to marinate at room temperature for 30 minutes, or up to a day, covered, in the fridge.

When getting ready to serve, whizz together all the ingredients for the garlic sauce with a hand-held blender or in a food processor until well blended. Set aside. Mix together the ingredients for the rainbow salad in a separate bowl.

Prepare a charcoal barbecue or preheat a gas barbecue until hot. Alternatively, preheat a griddle pan on the hob over a high heat. Thread the vegetables onto skewers and grill on the barbecue for 2–4 minutes or 3–5 minutes on the griddle pan, or longer if needed in either case, turning frequently to cook evenly on all sides.

Serve the aubergine in flatbreads with the hummus and harissa, along with the garlic sauce and the rainbow salad.

VE Opt for vegan yogurt and agave syrup
for the sauce.
GF Use gluten-free flatbreads or omit.

Green Crêpe Cake with Homemade Chocolate Spread and Chia Jam

MAKES 1 CAKE/SERVES 4–6

GREEN CRÊPE MIXTURE
200g spelt or plain flour
pinch of salt
400ml plant-based or dairy milk
3 eggs or egg replacers like aquafaba
2 handfuls of fresh spinach
vegetable oil, for frying

HOMEMADE CHOCOLATE SPREAD
200g raw hazelnuts
100g quality organic chocolate (70% cocoa), in pieces

CHIA JAM
200g raspberries, strawberries or other berries
1 tablespoon agave syrup
3 tablespoons water
2 tablespoons chia seeds

CHOCOLATE AND MASCARPONE CREAM
200g homemade chocolate spread
350g mascarpoone

TOPPINGS:
roasted hazelnuts
1 teaspoon raw cacao powder or cocoa powder

Pancakes or crêpes are the perfect picnic or potluck food, easily prepared at home. They can be used both as savoury-filled crêpes or as the base for a crêpe cake that you can assemble wherever you are, with the addition of delicious layer fillings such as homemade chocolate spread mixed with a creamy mascarpone or cashew cream and chia jam that you bring with you in sealed containers – in a flash you have an impressive cake. You can easily prepare the pancakes and the fillings a day ahead. These crêpes are made with the addtion of spinach, turning them vibrantly green!

For the chocolate spread, preheat the oven to 200°C/gas mark 6 and roast the hazelnuts for 10 minutes. Let them cool and place the hazelnuts in a clean towel. Fold the towel over the hazelnuts and twist the end to make a little sack, and rub the hazelnuts from the outside of the towel with your hands, so that the skins easily come off the nuts. Open the sack and place the hazelnuts in a food processor (save a few for decoration), pulse for 5 minutes and stop to scrape down the mixture from the edges of the processor in between.

In a small saucepan, melt the chocolate bar, let it cool slightly and pour into the hazelnut butter. Blend together.

For the chia jam, blend the ingredients together in a food processor. Transfer to a sterile jar and place in the fridge overnight. The chia jam keeps for 1 week in the fridge.

For the chocolate and mascarpone cream, mix the ingredients together with a spoon in a small bowl. Transfer to a sealed container and store in the fridge.

For the crêpes, blend the ingredients, except the oil, into a smooth mixture. Heat up a frying pan and add a drizzle of vegetable oil. Pour in the crêpe batter to make a round pancake with a diameter of 12–15cm. Fry until the pancake has firmed, then flip it over and fry the other side. There should be enough mixture to make 6 pancakes. Transfer to a plate and repeat until the batter is finished. Store the pancakes, sealed, in the fridge if you are not making the cake straightaway.

To make the cake, organise your workplace with one plate (or cake stand) in front of you, with the layer fillings and toppings within reach. Place a pancake on the plate and spread with the chocolate and mascarpone cream. Add another pancake and spread the chia jam, and another pancake and spread with chocolate and mascarpone cream again. Repeat until the last pancake. Top with chocolate and mascarpone cream, dust with cacao powder and decorate with hazelnuts.

Tip
Use ready roasted hazelnuts as a shortcut for the homemade chocolate spread.

VE Use vegan egg replacer.
GF Use a gluten free flour.

8. PLATED

For an intimate dinner, carefully prepared and plated dishes can
feel more special and less distracting than a buffet of sharing dishes.
Here is a selection of mains that balance texture and flavour
in each individual serving, where creamy meets crispy, smoky meets
fresh and sweet meets savoury. Let's get creative!

Smoky Shiitake with Pea Farrotto and Chai Tea Sauce

SERVES 4

PEA FARROTTO:
100g peas, fresh or frozen
600ml vegetable stock
olive oil or butter, for frying
3 garlic cloves, minced
220g semi-pearled farro
300ml white wine
50ml olive oil
70g Parmesan, grated, or rawmesan (see page 28), plus extra to serve
salt and freshly ground black pepper, to taste

SMOKY SHIITAKE:
1 tablespoon ghee or olive oil
½ teaspoon liquid smoke (optional)
300g shiitake mushrooms (or use oyster mushrooms or portobello), sliced
1 teaspoon toasted sesame oil
salt and freshly ground black pepper, to taste

CHAI TEA SAUCE:
200ml chai tea
½ teaspoon honey or agave syrup
salt and freshly ground black pepper, to taste

Peas and mushrooms are both fantastic ingredients and they complement each other perfectly in this dish. Not just highly versatile in cooking, peas are also rich in plant-based protein. And while mushrooms have been valued for their medicinal properties throughout history, it's their powerful umami flavour that is the winning quality in a plant-based diet.

These mushrooms are fried with half a teaspoon of liquid smoke, an ingredient used in gastronomic cooking. Liquid smoke is available in speciality cooking shops and online. Teas are essentially aromatic herbs and flowers and, when used in cooking, they add a beautiful and subtle flavour. Here, a sweet Chai tea is used to complement the savoury shiitake and farotto. You can also make the sauce with Earl Grey or Lapsang Souchong, the latter adds an extra smoky flavour to the sauce.

To make the pea farotto, put the green peas in a blender with 100ml of the stock and mix to a coarse, crumbly texture, or mash together with a fork in a bowl. Set aside.

Heat a saucepan over a medium-high heat. Add a drizzle of olive oil or a little butter and fry the garlic for a few seconds. Add the farro and fry, stirring, for 1–2 minutes. Stir in the wine and the rest of the vegetable stock and bring to the boil, then reduce the heat to low and simmer gently for 35–40 minutes, stirring frequently. Taste to see if the farro is tender, and if not, cook for a little longer.

Add the pea purée, olive oil and Parmesan or rawmesan and stir to mix, then season to taste with salt and pepper. Turn off the heat and cover the pan with a lid, then reheat just before serving.

Heat a frying pan over a medium-high heat. Add the ghee or olive oil and liquid smoke and fry the mushrooms for 2 minutes without stirring. Then fry, stirring, for a further 2–3 minutes or until the excess moisture has evaporated. Drizzle with the toasted sesame oil and season to taste with salt and pepper.

Remove the mushrooms and quickly pour the chai tea into the pan, whisking to combine the remaining flavours of the mushrooms with the tea. Add the honey or agave syrup and whisk it into the sauce. Taste and adjust with salt and pepper.

Serve the pea farrotto topped with the mushrooms and a drizzle of the chai tea sauce. You can top with extra Parmesan or rawmesan, if you like.

VE Opt for olive oil for frying and rawmesan.
GF Use brown rice or buckwheat instead of farro, adjusting the cooking times of the grains according to the packet instructions.

Caramelised Fennel Chops with Pumpkin Purée

SERVES 4

PUMPKIN PURÉE:
1 small (about 300g) pumpkin or
    butternut squash, halved, seeds and
    membrane removed
40ml olive oil
salt and freshly ground black pepper

4 small fennel bulbs, fronds and the
    rougher outer layer cut off
2 garlic cloves, minced
2 tablespoons olive oil
1 tablespoon balsamic vinegar
1 teaspoon ground fennel seeds
1 teaspoon thyme leaves
olive oil, for frying
1½ tablespoons coconut sugar
⅓ teaspoon salt
fresh thyme sprigs, to serve

RED WINE SAUCE
100ml red wine
1 tablespoon olive oil
salt and freshly ground black pepper,
    to taste

Caramelising vegetables adds extra gloss and char to the juicy flavours. This plate combines the sweetness of pumkin purée with garlic and balsamic glazed fennel chops. Keep the stem of the fennel during the cooking to hold the fennel together in a 'chop', though discard it when you eat. I love the simple way of making this quick sauce, adding liquid to the pan to absorb the residues of caramelisation - no flavour is wasted.

Preheat the oven to 160°C/gas mark 3. Place the pumpkin in an ovenproof dish. Roast for 50 minutes to 1 hour. Remove from the oven (but keep the oven on) and scrape the flesh out and transfer to a food processor. Blend with the olive oil and taste and adjust with salt and pepper.

Quarter the fennels lengthways, including the stem. Mix the garlic, olive oil, balsamic vinegar, fennel seeds and thyme in a small bowl.

Heat a big frying pan and add a generous drizzle of olive oil. Add the coconut sugar and salt and stir for a minute, lower the heat and place the pieces of fennel, cut-side down without overlapping, in the pan (fry in two batches). Cook the fennel until it's transparent and golden – 2–3 minutes on each side. When the fennel is cooked and golden, remove from the pan (but don't wash the pan up) and place in a bowl and drizzle with the garlic mixture.

Line a baking tray with baking paper and roast the fennel in the preheated oven for 8–10 minutes.

Meanwhile, reheat the pan that you used to caramelise the fennel, pour in the red wine and olive oil. Whisk the liquid and combine with the caramelised residue in the pan, infusing the sauce with flavour. Season to taste.

When the fennel is roasted, quickly reheat the pumpkin purée in a little pan and serve with the fennel on a plate. Drizzle over a spoonful of the red wine sauce and top with thyme sprigs.

VE ✓
GF ✓

Hot and Smoky Seitan Bangers with Red Cabbage Cider Confit and Green Mash

SERVES 4

SERVES 4

SEITAN SAUSAGES:
ghee or olive oil, for frying
100g shiitake mushrooms, sliced
2 garlic cloves, minced
200g drained canned beans, such as
    cannellini or haricot beans
1 tablespoon smoked paprika
3 tablespoons nutritional yeast or finely
    grated Parmesan
2 tablespoons shoyu soy or tamari sauce
400g seitan, drained
1 teaspoon liquid smoke
1 tablespoon chipotle paste or other
    chilli paste, or more to taste
50g rice flour
1 tablespoon olive oil
1 teaspoon dried oregano
½ teaspoon salt, or more to taste

RED CABBAGE CIDER CONFIT:
olive oil or ghee, for frying
1 red onion, thinly sliced
400g red cabbage, finely shredded
½ apple, cored and thinly sliced
1 teaspoon salt, or more to taste
300ml apple cider
300ml water
2 tablespoons red wine vinegar

FOR THE GREEN MASH:
400g broccoli florets
1 tablespoon tahini
2½ tablespoons olive oil
1 garlic clove, minced
1 teaspoon lemon juice
salt and freshly ground black pepper,
    to taste

MUSTARD MAYONNAISE:
100g mayonnaise
2½ tablespoons dijon mustard

pickled red onion, to serve (optional)

Serving a fancy sausage and mash plate is both fun and delicious. The sausages are made with seitan, which has the perfect texture and binding quality, spiced with smoked paprika, chipotle paste and liquid smoke for a robust flavour. They are served with broccoli mash along with a colourful cabbage confit and a mustard-enhanced mayo.

For the sausages, heat a frying pan over a medium-high heat. Add a little ghee or drizzle of olive oil and fry the shiitake with the garlic for about 7–8 minutes until they have shrunk in size and the excess liquid has reduced, stirring to avoid burning.

Transfer with all the remaining sausage ingredients to a food processor and whizz until smooth. Taste and adjust the seasoning with salt and chipotle paste if needed. Shape into 8–10 sausages. Wrap each sausage in foil or clingfilm and chill in the fridge for 1 hour or up to 24 hours.

Meanwhile, make the red cabbage cider confit. Heat a frying pan that has a lid over a medium-high heat. Add a generous drizzle of oil or equivalent quantity of ghee and fry the onion, stirring, for 3–4 minutes. Add the cabbage and fry, stirring, for 5 minutes. Stir in all the remaining confit ingredients and cover the pan with the lid. Reduce the heat and simmer gently for 35–40 minutes, stirring occasionally.

Meanwhile, make the green mash. Steam the broccoli florets for 4 minutes. Transfer to a food processor and blend until smooth with the rest of the ingredients. Taste and adjust with salt and pepper.

Preheat the oven to 180°C/gas mark 4. Unwrap the sausages, place on a baking tray and bake for 30 minutes until golden brown, turning occasionally. Alternatively, heat a frying pan to a medium-high heat and fry the sausages for a few minutes, turning frequently, until golden brown.

While the sausages are cooking, mix the mayonnaise and mustard together in a small bowl. Quickly reheat the green mash. Serve the sausages with the green mash, red cabbage cider confit, mustard mayonnaise and pickled red onion, if you like.

VE Opt for nutritional yeast, olive oil
for frying and vegan mayonnaise.
GF This recipe is not gluten-free.

Tip
You can also make super-delicious croquettes with the same mixture by rolling the sausages in panko breadcrumbs and frying in the same way as for the Croquettes on page 165. Another way to serve the sausages is in hot dog buns, substituting coleslaw for the confit, or try serving the sausages with chutney and top-quality ketchup. You can also buy plant-based sausage skins to stuff, in stores specialising in vegan food or online.

Croquettes with Mustard Mayo

SERVES 4

CROQUETTES:
800g medium-small waxy potatoes
3 organic egg yolks
100ml dairy or plant-based milk
70g Parmesan or rawmesan (see page
    28), finely grated
1 teaspoon salt
¼ teaspoon ground white pepper
3 medium organic eggs
100g flour of choice
100g panko breadcrumbs
vegetable oil, for frying

MUSTARD MAYONNAISE:
200g mayonnaise
1 tablespoon Dijon mustard

TO SERVE:
4 small slices of sourdough, toasted
pickled red onion
avocado slices
fresh herbs such as chives, dill or
    parsley (optional)

Croquettes are a star turn when it comes to texture, with their crusty exterior and soft, creamy inside, but forget the artificial taste of processed fast-food croquettes - these upmarket versions are in another league.

Mustard mayo is the ideal accompaniment for the crispy balls, along with rustic sourdough toast, but you can easily serve the croquettes with just a simple green salad. The croquettes are also delicious with a garlic sauce or garlic butter with fresh herbs.

For the croquettes, preheat the oven to 180°C/gas mark 4. Line a baking tray with baking paper. Place the potatoes on the lined tray and bake for 50 minutes. Remove from the oven and leave to cool, then cut in half and scoop out the flesh, discarding the skins. Mash in a bowl. Whisk together the egg yolks and milk and then stir into the mash with the Parmesan or rawmesan, salt and white pepper. Form the mixture into oval-shaped balls, place on a tray and leave to chill in the fridge for 1-2 hours.

Preheat the oven to 110°C/gas mark ¼. Line a baking tray with baking paper. Mix the mayonnaise and mustard together in a small bowl.

Beat together the eggs in one bowl, add the flour to a second bowl and the breadcrumbs to another. Add a generous drizzle of oil to a frying pan and heat over a medium-high heat. First roll the balls in flour, then dip in the beaten egg and then roll in the breadcrumbs to coat. Fry, in batches, for 3-4 minutes, turning regularly for even cooking. Remove from the oil and drain on kitchen paper to absorb the excess oil. Transfer each fried croquette to the lined tray and keep warm in the oven while you finish frying the remainder.

Serve the warm croquettes with the mustard mayonnaise, along with the sourdough toast, pickled red onion and avocado and a few herbs.

VE Use vegan mayonnaise, rawmesan, plant-based milk, and omit the egg yolks and eggs altogether. Skip rolling the croquettes in flour and egg, go straight to coating with panko before frying.
GF Use gluten-free flour, breadcrumbs and toasted rustic gluten-free bread.

Miso-glazed Aubergine with Furikake Rice

SERVES 4

200g Japanese or sushi rice

2 small aubergines

sesame or vegetable oil, for frying

sesame seeds, black or white or a mix,
    for sprinkling

FURIKAKE (MAKES ABOUT 200G):

1 ready-toasted nori sheet, ½ very finely
    chopped, ½ cut into thin, short strips
    and reserved for garnish

70g white sesame seeds, toasted

70g black sesame seeds

1 teaspoon shichimi togarashi or dried
    chilli flakes

2 tablespoons shoyu soy or tamari sauce

2 tablespoons coconut sugar

MISO GLAZE:

100g red miso paste or use another miso
    of your choice

2 tablespoons mirin

1 tablespoon agave syrup or maple syrup

TO SERVE (OPTIONAL):

Japanese Pickles (see page 129)

Wakame Salad (see page 129)

Carrot ribbons, to garnish

This popular Japanese dish, known as nasu dengaku, dates back hundreds of years and demonstrates how aubergine magically transforms from drab to delicious under the grill. The miso glaze adds a savoury hit without using salt itself, and is contrasted by sweetness from the agave or maple syrup for an extra-tasty result. When mixing the glaze, taste and adjust the balance of savoury and sweet, adding more syrup, if needed.

To make the furikake, put the finely chopped nori in a food processor with all the remaining furikake ingredients and whizz until well combined. Transfer to a sterilised jar, seal and keep in the fridge for up a week.

Rinse and cook the rice according to the instructions on page 16 (onigiri).

Meanwhile, cut the aubergines in half lengthways and make a crisscross of cuts in the flesh of each half. Put all the ingredients for the miso glaze in a bowl and whisk until combined.

Preheat the oven on the grill setting or to 240°C/gas mark 9 or its highest setting, or preheat the grill to high. Line a baking tray with baking paper. Heat a frying pan that has a lid over a medium-high heat. Add a drizzle of oil and fry the rounded side of the aubergine halves for 3–4 minutes until the skin is shrivelled. Flip the aubergine halves over, cut-side down, cover the pan with the lid and fry for 3 minutes. Transfer the aubergine halves, cut-side up, to the lined tray and brush generously with the miso glaze. Grill for 3–4 minutes or until the glaze has caramelised.

Sprinkle the cooked rice with sesame seeds and 2 tablespoons of the furikake (and put extra furikake on the table) and garnish with the reserved nori strips and carrot ribbons. Serve with the aubergine, along with the pickles and wakame salad, if you like.

VE Make your own furikake or look for tuna-free furikake if
buying ready-made.
GF Opt for tamari sauce.

Using miso

Miso paste is made by fermenting soya beans, or sometimes rice or other grains, resulting in an intensely savoury, naturally salty flavouring that can be added to either liquids or fat and used in marinades and sauces or soups and stews as you would soy sauce. Varieties of miso range from light to dark, the darker the stronger the flavour, with white miso being mild enough to be used in desserts.

Faux Fishcakes with Almond Sesame Dip

SERVES 4

ALMOND SESAME DIP:
2 tablespoons almond butter
1½ tablespoons toasted sesame oil
1½ tablespoons shoyu soy or
    tamari sauce
2 tablespoons fresh lime juice
1 teaspoon honey or agave syrup

FAUX FISHCAKES:
250g smoked tofu
2½ tablespoons shoyu soy or
    tamari sauce
a handful of coriander
1½ tablespoons finely chopped seaweed –
    I use nori or hijiki, but any kind will do
1 teaspoon honey or agave syrup
2 spring onions, chopped
2 garlic cloves, crushed
1 tablespoon sriracha sauce
2 teaspoons finely grated fresh ginger
200g cooked brown rice
salt, to taste
sesame or vegetable oil, for frying

TO SERVE:
300g mixed vegetables and fruit, such as
    carrot, cucumber and radishes, peeled
    and/or deseeded as appropriate and
    cut into bite-sized pieces
drizzles of sweet rice vinegar
    (sushi vinegar)
sesame seeds, for sprinkling

This recipe makes a great dinner dish and has been a favourite in our house for many years. The combination of seaweed and smoked tofu gives the cakes a seafood-like flavour, with coriander, ginger and soy adding an Asian-style freshness and fragrance. The cakes are made even more scrumptious by being dunked in an almond sesame dip.

Whizz together all the ingredients for the almond sesame dip with a hand-held blender in a jug until well blended.

Put all the ingredients for the faux fishcakes, except the oil, in a food processor and whizz together until well combined. Taste and adjust the seasoning with salt. Shape the mixture into 12 small cakes, place on a tray and chill in the fridge for 30 minutes. Preheat the oven to 110°C/gas mark ¼. Line a baking tray with baking paper.

Heat a frying pan over a medium heat. Add a drizzle of oil and fry the cakes in batches, a couple at a time with ample space between the cakes, for 2–3 minutes on each side until golden brown. Transfer the fried cakes to the lined tray and keep warm in the oven while you finish frying the remainder.

Divide the cakes between plates and arrange the cut vegetables decoratively and drizzle with a little sweet rice vinegar. Drizzle with the almond sesame dip and sprinkle with sesame seeds.

VE Opt for agave syrup.
GF Opt for tamari sauce.

Baked Polenta with Caponata and Roasted Beets

SERVES 4

ROASTED BEETS:

4 small beetroots, scrubbed and
    quartered
1 tablespoon balsamic vinegar
1 tablespoon olive oil
salt and freshly ground black pepper

POLENTA:

1 litre water
250g polenta (not the quick-cook type)
3 tablespoons olive oil
70g Parmesan or rawmesan (see
    page 28), grated
salt and freshly ground black pepper,
    to taste

CAPONATA:

olive oil, for frying
1 aubergine, diced
2 celery sticks, finely chopped
2 red peppers, cored, deseeded and cut
    into small pieces
2 best-quality tomatoes, chopped
2 garlic cloves, crushed
1 red onion, finely chopped
50g black olives, halved and pitted
a handful of flat-leaf parsley,
    finely chopped
2 teaspoons dried oregano
150ml water
200ml tomato sauce
50ml red wine vinegar
2–3 Medjool dates, pitted and finely
    chopped (or a handful of dried fruit,
    finely chopped)
2 teaspoons salt
¼ teaspoon freshly ground
    black pepper

This meal is the perfect Sunday lunch or dinner, especially served with a good red wine or a fine cider. Polenta, originating from Italy, is made from cornmeal and traditionally cooked by lengthy stirring on the hob. It's becoming increasingly popular to bake polenta in the oven, which means less stirring, but the baking process also adds extra flavour. The polenta is baked until firm. I use cookie moulds to cut out a round portion for each plate. You can also cut the polenta in squares or if you would like a creamy polenta bake only for 30 minutes. I've topped it here with another Italian classic - caponata - and roasted beets.

Preheat the oven to 180°C/gas mark 4. Line a shallow oven-proof dish with baking paper. In a bowl, toss the beets with olive oil, balsamic vinegar and salt and pepper. Set aside.

To make the polenta, bring the water to the boil in a large saucepan. Slowly pour in the polenta while whisking vigorously to avoid lumps forming. When the mixture is smooth, reduce the heat and simmer for 5 minutes, whisking constantly. Stir in the olive oil and Parmesan or Rawmesan, then taste and adjust the seasoning with salt and pepper. Pour the polenta into the lined tin and bake for 40 minutes, for a firm polenta. For a creamy polenta, roast for 25-30 minutes.

Place the beets on a separate tray in the oven at the same time and roast for 40 minutes, check their doneness and extend the roasting a few minutes, if needed.

Meanwhile, make the caponata. Heat a frying pan over a medium-high heat. Add a generous drizzle of olive oil and fry the vegetables, olives and herbs together for 15-20 minutes, stirring frequently, until fragrant and golden. Stir in the water, tomato sauce, vinegar and dates and season with salt and pepper. Reduce the heat to low and leave the caponata to simmer gently for 20 minutes, stirring occasionally to avoid it catching on the base of the pan.

Remove the polenta from the oven and if you opted for a firm polenta, cut into portions using a knife or cookie mould. If you opted for a creamy polenta, use a big spoon to scoop the polenta onto the plate. Top with the caponata and roasted beets.

VE Opt for rawmesan.
GF ✓

9. SWEET ENDINGS

This chapter could just as easily have been titled 'Sweet Beginnings', as in my home country
of Sweden it is a traditional part of everyday life that we get together and share a sweet treat,
a custom we call fika. So for my fellow Swedes in particular, I have included a recipe for babka,
which is similar in flavour to our traditional Swedish cinnamon rolls but a bit heavier on the spice!
For the ideal dessert for warmer days, chill out in style with my exotic freezer mango cheesecake
or some intriguing-tasting and -looking homemade ice cream with black sesame seeds.
But if you're wanting something cosy and comforting instead, indulge in the chai-flavoured
carrot cake or waffles with berries and caramel sauce.
For a light and delicate dessert, my panna cotta made with coconut cream
and green matcha tea powder will fit the bill perfectly.

Matcha Coconut Panna Cotta

SERVES 4

PANNACOTTA:

½ teaspoon agar agar powder

2 tablespoons water

2 teaspoons green matcha tea powder,
plus extra for sprinkling to decorate
(optional – choose from the other
flavouring options)

400ml coconut cream

2 tablespoons honey or agave syrup

¼ teaspoon vanilla extract or 1 vanilla
pod, split lengthways and seeds
scraped out

FLAVOURING OPTIONS:

2 tablespoons puréed mango

1 teaspoon freshly brewed strong coffee

1 teaspoon finely grated lime zest

1 teaspoon rum

2 tablespoons puréed raspberries

1 teaspoon rose water or rose syrup or
other flower extract

TO SERVE:

agave syrup

sprinkle of bee pollen (optional)

black sesame seeds or toasted
crushed nuts

This dessert literally melts in your mouth, as its texture is so refined and silky. While traditional panna cotta is made with dairy and gelatine, this version combines coconut cream and agar agar to create a fully plant-based alternative. I've added green matcha tea powder for an interesting twist, but you can skip it to create a classic white panna cotta if you prefer. It's easy to make variations of this dessert by simply substituting another flavour for the matcha – see the ingredient list for suggestions. You can of course use dairy cream instead of coconut cream.

Mix the agar agar powder with the water and matcha powder in a small bowl until well blended. Place a small saucepan over a low heat. Add the agar agar mixture and all the remaining panna cotta ingredients, including your choice of flavouring, and simmer gently for 1–2 minutes. Pour the warm mixture into four moulds (I use muffin moulds but soufflé dishes or other round small moulds will also work) and allow to cool. Chill in the fridge for 1½ hours. Remove from the fridge and invert each mould in turn onto a serving plate, then lift away the mould to reveal the panna cotta.

Serve with a drizzle of agave syrup and a pinch of crunchy toppings like sprinkles of bee pollen, black sesame seeds or toasted crushed nuts.

VE Opt for agave syrup.
GF ✓

Tip

Matcha powder varies greatly in quality and price. The finest matcha is handpicked and designated as 'ceremonial grade', the type used in traditional Japanese tea ceremonies, whereas cheaper and lower-quality matcha can be more bitter and 'off' in taste. So look for the ceremonial grade variety when buying matcha.

Sweet Tahini Babka

SERVES 6

120ml warm (not hot) plant-based or
    dairy milk
2 teaspoons fast-action dried yeast
50g coconut sugar
¼ teaspoon salt
250g spelt or plain flour, plus extra
    for dusting
1 large organic egg
1 teaspoon vanilla extract
70g butter, softened, or 70ml olive oil

ORANGE TAHINI CHOCOLATE SPREAD:

130g coconut sugar
50ml tahini
4 tablespoons raw cacao or cocoa powder
2 teaspoons ground cinnamon
60g butter, softened, or 70ml olive oil,
    plus extra for greasing
pinch of salt
1 tablespoons grated orange zest

SWEET GLAZE:

1 tablespoon honey or agave syrup
2 tablespoons water

Babka is Polish for grandmother and also the name of a classic Jewish sweet yeast bread. My first encounter with babka was in a Jewish café in Amsterdam, and it was instant love because it was so delicious and reminiscent of the cinnamon rolls of my childhood in Sweden. Popular fillings for babka are chocolate and cinnamon, but for this version I've added tahini for a sesame twist, which gives the sweet spread a slightly savoury, nutty edge. Traditional babka recipes call for butter, making for a lovely rich taste, but you can use olive oil instead with excellent results and egg replacer for a vegan babka.

Whisk together the warm milk, yeast and a pinch of the coconut sugar in a small bowl. Leave to stand for about 10 minutes to allow the yeast to activate – you'll see it becoming foamy on the surface.

Mix together the remainder of the coconut sugar, the salt and flour in a mixing bowl, or in the bowl of a stand mixer fitted with the paddle attachment. In a separate bowl, beat together the egg and vanilla extract. Add the egg mixture to the flour while mixing constantly with your hands or with the mixer on low speed until incorporated. Then add the yeast mixture and keep kneading while you gradually add the butter or olive oil, switching to the dough hook if using a mixer. Continue kneading on a floured work surface, if kneading by hand, until the dough is smooth. Grease a bowl with butter or olive oil, add the dough and cover with a clean tea towel. Leave to rise in the kitchen for 2 hours.

Meanwhile, line a 1.5 litre loaf tin with baking paper. Mix together all the ingredients for the orange tahini chocolate spread in a bowl and set aside.

Roll the dough out on a work surface lightly dusted with flour into a large rectangle, 3–5mm thick. Spread with an even layer of the orange tahini chocolate spread. Starting from one longer side, roll up the dough into a long roll. Slice the roll in half lengthways. Keeping the cut sides facing upwards, wind the two long pieces of dough around each other to form a twisted rope, then place in the greased loaf tin. Tuck in the ends of the dough to neaten. Cover with the tea towel and leave the babka to rise in the kitchen for 30 minutes to 1 hour.

Meanwhile, preheat the oven to 180°C/gas mark 4. Put the honey or agave syrup and water for the glaze in a small saucepan and bring to the boil, stirring. Reduce the heat and simmer for a couple of minutes, then set aside.

Bake the babka for 30 minutes or until golden brown. Remove from the oven and brush with the glaze. Leave to cool in the tin before slicing and serving.

VE Opt for plant-based milk, olive oil, vegan egg
replacer and agave syrup.
GF The babka is not gluten-free.

Black Sesame Ice Cream with Lime and Sea Salt

MAKES ABOUT 1 LITRE

800ml coconut cream

2 tablespoons lime juice

150g coconut sugar

100g black sesame seeds

100g raw cashew nuts, soaked in water
for 2–4 hours and drained

1½ teaspoons vanilla extract

½ teaspoon sea salt

1 tablespoon arrowroot

CHOCOLATE DRIZZLE:

50g good-quality organic dark chocolate,
broken into pieces, or 2 tablespoons
cocoa powder

2 tablespoons coconut oil

1 teaspoon agave syrup

TO SERVE:

cones (optional)

a handful of toasted nuts, crushed

Big in Japan but still a relatively rare sight in ice cream parlours in the West, this black sesame ice cream is certainly something else! Think ice-cold creamy and sweet tahini and you're not far from imagining the taste. You can add a touch of edible charcoal powder to the ingredients for a true black colour, but personally I love the minimal natural grey beige look of this ice cream with the tiny speckles of black sesame seeds.

Put all the ingredients for the ice cream in a blender or food processor and whizz until smooth – there will be tiny dots of black sesame seed visible in the mixture.

Transfer the ice-cream mixture to a bowl, cover and chill in the fridge for 30 minutes. Churn the mixture in an ice-cream maker for 25 minutes or until firm and frozen. Transfer the ice cream to a freezer-proof container and freeze for 30 minutes before serving. It will keep in the freezer for two months.

Meanwhile, put the ingredients for the chocolate drizzle in a small saucepan and heat gently, stirring, until melted and well blended.

To serve, scoop the ice cream into cones or small bowls, drizzle with or dip into the chocolate drizzle and sprinkle with or dip into the crushed nuts.

VE Use vegan chocolate.

GF Omit the cones and serve in bowls or cups.

Ginger and Hibiscus Poached Pears with Ice Cream

SERVES 4

4 firm pears, peeled but stalks intact
1 litre strong hibiscus tea (let it steep for
    10 minutes at least)
1 tablespoon puréed fresh ginger
1 teaspoon puréed lemongrass (optional)
2 tablespoons agave syrup
1 teaspoon vanilla extract

TO SERVE:
ice cream, mascarpone or Whipped
    Coconut Cream (see page 185)
sprinkles of black sesame seeds

Poached pears look and taste stunning and yet are simple to prepare. Here they are infused with hibiscus tea, aromatic fresh ginger and hibiscus tea during the process. Serve it with vanilla ice cream, mascarpone or Coconut Whipped Cream (see page 185).

—

Put the pears in a saucepan. Fill the saucepan with hibiscus tea and add the puréed ginger, puréed lemongrass, agave syrup and vanilla extract. Bring to the boil, then reduce the heat and simmer for 30 minutes. Turn off the heat but keep the pears in the syrup until ready to serve. The pears can be poached up to 2 days in advance, then cooled and kept, tightly covered, in the fridge. Reheat gently before serving.

Carefully remove the pears from the syrup and serve with ice cream or mascarpone. Sprinkle with black sesame seeds.

VE Use vegan ice cream.
GF ✓

No-Bake Mango Cheesecake

SERVES 6

BASE:

250g mixed toasted or raw nuts, such as
    almonds and cashew nuts, unsalted
150g Medjool dates, pitted and
    roughly chopped
½ teaspoon sea salt

TOPPING:

100g coconut oil
100g mango pulp
2 tablespoons agave syrup
250g raw cashew nuts, soaked in water
    for 2–4 hours, then drained
1 teaspoon lime juice

Semi-frozen no-bake cakes are my go-to choice for hot summer days, and this recipe is both vegan and gluten free for maximum flexibility. The natural sweet stickiness of dates binds the nuts together for the base and adding a little salt gives it a slight caramel quality. The smooth, juicy mango filling makes a delicious contrast to the nutty base. Coconut oil is often used in raw cakes because it readily solidifies at low temperatures, so chilling the cake firms the filling nicely.

To make the base, put the nuts in a food processor and pulse until coarsely ground. Add the dates and salt and whizz until the mixture is sticky and grainy. Press onto the base of a 15–20cm springform cake tin to form an even layer.

To make the topping, add the coconut oil, in small quantities at a time, to the food processor with the remaining filling ingredients and whizz until well blended. Pour over the base and smooth the surface with a spatula. Freeze the cheesecake for a minimum of an hour or until firm.

To serve, release the cheesecake from the tin and leave to stand at room temperature for 20 minutes.

VE ✓
GF ✓

Sweet Mess with Salted Caramel

When you are catering for a number of people, serving an easy dessert gives you more time to enjoy being social. Here, simple waffles are topped with fruit and berries, creamy ricotta and drizzled with caramel sauce. You can serve whipped coconut cream or ice cream instead of ricotta.

SERVES 6
300g ricotta or Whipped
    Coconut Cream, optional
6 Waffles, freshly made
200g fresh berries or pieces of freshly
    cut fruit

SALTED CARAMEL
400ml coconut milk or other mik
150g coconut or brown sugar
2 tablespoons raw cacao powder
1 teaspoon vanilla essence
⅓ teaspoon salt and more to taste
1 teaspoon mild olive oil or coconut oil

To make the caramel sauce, whisk the ingredients together in a heavy-bottomed pan and bring to the boil, lower the heat and let the sauce simmer for 5 minutes while stirring. Set aside. Place the waffles on a serving plate and top with fruit and berries. Drizzle with caramel sauce and serve with ricotta.

VE Use coconut cream.
GF Make the waffles with gluten-free flour.

Whipped Coconut Cream

Whipped dairy cream is easily substituted with whipped coconut cream. Use a thick coconut cream, not the drinking variety of coconut milk.

SERVES 4
250ml coconut cream, refrigerated
1 tablespoon honey or agave syrup
1 teaspoon vanilla extract
½ teaspoon lemon juice

Whisk all the ingredients together. Place in the fridge until ready to serve.

VE ✓
GF ✓

Waffles

Crispy waffles are the perfect companion to creamy mascarpone or whipped coconut cream and berries. These waffles are egg free and suitable for vegans.

SERVES 4
3 tablespoons mild olive oil, plus extra
    for brushing
300ml plant-based or dairy milk
200g spelt or plain flour or gluten-
    free flour
1 teaspoon baking powder
¼ teaspoon of salt
1 teaspoon vanilla extract
3 tablespoons coconut or brown sugar

Mix all the ingredients together in a food processor. Preheat the oven to 110°C/gas mark ¼. Line a baking tray with baking paper. Preheat a waffle maker. Brush the waffle maker with olive oil, then cook the waffles in batches, following the manufacturer's instructions, until golden brown and crisp. Transfer the fried waffles to the lined tray and keep warm in the oven while you finish frying the remainder.

VE ✓
GF Make the waffles using gluten-free flour.

Chai Carrot Cake with Lime and Rose Icing

SERVES 6

coconut oil or butter, for greasing
175g spelt flour
¾ teaspoon baking powder
¾ teaspoon bicarbonate of soda
¾ teaspooon salt
1 teaspoon ground cinnamon
½ teaspoon ground cardamom
½ teaspoon ground ginger
¼ teaspoon ground nutmeg
pinch of freshly ground black pepper
150g coconut sugar
130ml olive oil
50ml agave syrup
1 teaspoon vanilla extract
2 medium organic eggs
120g carrots, finely grated

LIME AND ROSE ICING:

150g cream cheese or vegan crème
    fraîche or white cashew cream
1 teaspoon vanilla extract
1 teaspoon fresh lime juice
1½ tablespoons agave syrup
½ tablespoon rose water (optional)

TO DECORATE

pomegranate seeds
rose petals, fresh or dried
hazlenuts or pistachio nuts

I have always had a soft spot for carrot cakes and this comforting spiced version is a regular on the table at home. Indian chai flavours of cinnamon, cardamom and nutmeg work beautifully in baking and here they bring a warmth to the juicy carrots. The sharp, floral-tasting frosting provides a delicious cool contrast to the spicy cake. You can extend the Indian theme by serving the cake with Mango Lassi (see page 33) or Golden Milk Latte (see page 33).

Preheat the oven to 180°C/gas mark 4. Grease a round 20cm cake tin with coconut oil or butter, line the base and sides with baking paper and then grease the paper.

Put all the ingredients for the lime and rose frosting in a bowl and whisk together until light and creamy. Cover the bowl and refrigerate until ready to assemble the cake.

Sift the flour, baking powder, bicarbonate of soda, salt, spices and pepper into a mixing bowl and mix well. In another bowl, whisk together the coconut sugar, olive oil, agave syrup and vanilla extract. Add the eggs one by one (or, if using egg replacer, half at a time) while whisking constantly. Pour the oil and egg mixture into the dry mixture and mix together, then fold in the grated carrot.

Pour the cake batter into the prepared cake tin, level the surface, and bake for 45 minutes or until a thin skewer inserted into the centre of the cake comes out clean. Remove from the oven and leave to cool for 30 minutes in the tin. Turn the cake out of the tin and place on a serving plate. Spread the frosting over the top of the cake and sprinkle with pomegranate seeds and rose petals and nuts.

VE Opt for vegan egg replacer and vegan natural cream cheese and vegan crème fraîche
GF The cake is not gluten free.

INDEX

Thanks

To my family Natal, Nova and Evan, and to my table guests, friends and helpers,
Santouscha Tjietaman, Bensimon Van Leyen, Sarah Cheikh, Fleur Schouten, Marie Sophie,
Surf Avalon, Aïsha Zafirah, Geraldine Faureau, Paul Edouard Tastet, Tim Holdredge,
Fabio Bortolazzi, Imogen Visscher, Djenna Wallace, Manu, Suzanne, Jessica, Q Oijjevarr, Jesse
and Zanna Kalf, Willemijn Meijer, Yannick Steensma, Sam Hof, Haye Beeldman, Suze Boorsma,
Ulysis, Tisha Prins, Kesia Jorissen, Ryan Oijjevaar, Bo Oijjevaar, Floris Schmidt, Franky Howe,
Joris Perez, Silvan Arhem, Jaqueline Schouten, Juliette Kwikkers, Natalie Ilario, Jan,
Barbara and Norbert van Leyen, Gerard Bouwman and Thom Widdershoven.
An extra warm and special thanks to Olivia (@adelasterfoodtextures) for our Midsummer
celebration on Bohusläns coast in Sweden, and to the Swedes: Alexandra Toftesjö,
Moa Hallmyr Lewis, Maria Andreassen, Kristina Larsson and Edward Thorden.
A special namaste to my sister Leoni and Sekoya Yoga and Holistic Center for the friendship
through thick and thin, and not to forget for invaulable production assistance.
Warm thanks to Suus Slee from @foodbandits for lending props.

Huge thanks to my editor Sophie Allen, and Sarah Kyle at Kyle Books for invaluable
input and hard work with this book. Also to the copy editor Jo Richardson for translating my
swenglish (Swedish tinted English langugage) into flawless, english sentences.
And a big thanks to the talented production team for a beautiful finish on my photography.

Also thanks to my readers and Instagram followers for your invaluable support,
feedback and love. This book is for you! I never thought I would hear back from so many happy
eaters after Bowls of Goodness was published and it's now one of the reasons why I want to keep
making and share recipes, it's truly a rewarding feeling, knowing that the food is cooked and
enjoyed in homes all over the world. If you cook from this book and like to post your creation on
social media, feel free to tag me and use the hashtag #feastsofveg. I can't wait to see it.

Resources

My favourite set of ceramics (frequently) used in this book, is hand made
by AnneMieke Boots Ceramics, find her at www.annemiekebootsceramics.nl or
on Instagram @annemiekebootsceramics

These brands and creative friends of which products and services I relied on in the
making of this book, find them on instagram or their homepage: @foodbandits
@cultchakombucha @organicfoodforyou
@tallyho_offical, @debiologischenordermaarkt @knead_more_bread
@organicfoodforyou @sekoyacenter @letoile.store